CHANGING PATTERNS OF CASTE & CLASS RELATIONS IN SOUTH INDIA

Social Stratification and Social Mobility

Dr. L. THARA BHAI

Gian Publishing House

29/6 SHAKTI NAGAR • DELHI-110007 • INDIA

GIAN PUBLISHING HOUSE
29/6 Shakti Nagar, Delhi-110007

ISBN 81-212-0087-3

PRINTED IN INDIA
Published by Mrs. Gayatri Garg for Gian Publishing House, Delhi and Printed at Mohan Printing Corporation, Delhi.

PREFACE

The traditional stratification in Indian society was a caste oriented one in which caste and class used to synchronize. Subsequent to political Independence, this pattern has undergone radical changes resulting into the emergence of a new pattern of stratification in which class is given the primacy. It was this aspect of change in the stratification system that I wanted to analyse particularly when I came across some of the works of my guide Dr. Raj. Also I was fascinated by the dialectical approach he has been using in analysing social phenomena. Like him, I also felt that dialectical approach to the study of social stratification may be more fruitful in gaining insight than the functional approach. Mine is only a humble attempt to explain the problem of change in social stratification in our society.

The problem of the study and the method are stated in the first Chapter. The social structure of the selected villages are discussed in the second Chapter. The traditional caste stratification has been discussed in the third Chapter. Inter-caste and intra-caste relations and the changing value system are analysed in the fourth and fifth chapters. The emergent class stratification and intra-class and inter-class relations are discussed in the sixth and seventh chapters. The changing pattern of political, economic and occupational relations with reference to changing pattern of stratification are analysed in the eighth and ninth chapters. The theoretical abstractions that are derived from the study are brought together in the last chapter.

L. Thara Bhai

PREFACE

The traditional stratification of Indian society was [illegible] around caste in which [illegible] and [illegible] [illegible] Subsequent [illegible] political independence, the [illegible] [illegible] changes resulting into the [illegible] [illegible] [illegible] which [illegible] the [illegible] this aspect of change in the stratification system [illegible] [illegible] [illegible] [illegible] approach [illegible] [illegible] [illegible] [illegible] that [illegible] to the study of social stratification [illegible] insight than the [illegible] approach [illegible] [illegible] [illegible] the [illegible] [illegible] [illegible] [illegible]

The problem of the study and the method are [illegible] in the first Chapter. The social structure of the selected village is discussed in the second Chapter. The traditional [illegible] [illegible] has been discussed in the third Chapter. [illegible] and [illegible] [illegible] and of [illegible] [illegible] analysed in the [illegible] [illegible] [illegible] [illegible] [illegible] class and [illegible] [illegible] [illegible] in the sixth and seventh chapters. The [illegible] [illegible] of political, economic and occupational relations with [illegible] [illegible] [illegible] of [illegible] groups are analysed in the [illegible] and [illegible] chapters. The [illegible] of [illegible] [illegible] derived from the study are brought [illegible] [illegible] [illegible]

CONTENTS

CHAPTER ONE

INTRODUCTION

Stratification in some form or other is found in all societies and groups. Societies which are structured or found to have a particular order can be said to possess a stratification system.[1] In the most simple form, stratication can be regarded as a hierarchical arrangement of certain groups or categories. These groups or categories are composed of individuals. Individuals who belong to these groups are invested with powers in different measures corresponding to various strata to which they belong. Thus, each stratum in a stratification system represents a group or category of individuals who are invested with institutional positions or roles. In any hierarchical stratification system, the institutional positions or roles within the stratum at the apex involve a near monopoly in ownership or control over the scarce values which are necessary for social survival. Such ownership or control may also entail similar dominant positions in the derived social and cultural spheres. The institutional positions or roles of individuals belonging to the strata at the bottom are divested of any control or ownership over the scarce values necessary for social survival and instead these roles and social survival of incumbents of these roles in the lower strata are dependent on the roles and social survival of the incumbents in the upper strata. The incumbents of the institutional roles, irrespective of the strata to which they belong, "tend to some

extent transmit such positions to their children or to other persons who are seen as extensions of their premordial identity...".[2]

In societies having hierarchical stratification, individuals who possess the maximum control over scarce values of social survival are placed at the apex, followed by other strata possessing lesser degree of control or ownership till the lowest stratum is reached, in which the individuals who compose it do not possess any control or ownership over the scarce values of social survival. Such a pattern of stratification may synchronize with "a system of ranked statuses by which all members are placed in superior and inferior positions".[3] Thus a varying degree of status is a feature of stratification. In other words each group or category of individuals in a stratification system may acquire a particular status which differs from the others. As the system of "ranked statuses" is only a vicarious manifestation of the differential distribution pattern of the scarce values of social survival, it may be possible to understand the system of "ranked statuses" only in terms of the differential distribution pattern of scarce values among different strata.

Again the value system of a society or group plays an important role in maintaining and perpetuating the stratification system within it. As the stratification process varies from society to society, each society develops its own corresponding value system. One may agree with Parsons to the extent that "stratification in its valuational aspect is the ranking of unit in a social system in accordance with the standards of common value system".[4] But if we attempt to approach the problem of stratification from the normative angle alone, as has been done by Parsons and other functionalists, we will be mistaking trees for the wood. In order to place the problem of social stratification in the proper perspective, one has to approach the valuational aspect as a derivative of the differential distribution pattern of the scarce values of social survival.

Though social stratification is found in all fields of social relations, they are interdependent. This necessitates the study of social stratification "as a cluster of interdependent economic, political and other social relations"[5] in which stratification in

political and other social relations is to be analysed in terms of stratification in the field of economic relations.

In short the stratification system of a society is the 'pattern' or 'ordering' of social relations within that society.[6] Such ordering or patterning of relations involves the inequitable distribution of scarce values giving rise to a stratified system of economic divisions, the emergent normative and value system, and the patterns of conformity and non-conformity with the corresponding system of rewards and punishments.

As stratification system was central for growth, stability and instability in all societies it became focus for many sociological investigations. Depending on whether the concern is with change or no-change, various approaches to the study of stratification may, by and large, be classified into two categories of functional and dialectical approaches.

1. Functional Approach

Functional approach to the study of social stratification is based on the premise that the differentiation of roles and duties are inevitable in a society and consequently a hierarchical stratification is also inevitable. Without such a hierarchical system, no society can survive. Within this frame of reference, functionalists like Kingsley Davis[7] and Wilbert E. Moore[8] have attempted to provide a psychic interpretation to the phenomenon of stratification, by giving emphasis to roles and role evaluations of individual actors. Many like Arthur W. Korhanser[9], Richard Centres[10] and Parsons[11] have tried to explain the problem in terms of psychic factors like feelings, and subjective identification of the individual actors vis-a-vis their class positions.

Such a functional approach to the problem of stratification may be useful in understanding stability rather than instability, integration rather than disintegration. The predominance of functional approach in the study of social stratification in contemporary Sociology is probably due to the emergent concern "to preserve stability and integration so as to safeguard the

emergent differential distribution pattern of the economic scarce values of production in Western Societies".[12]

As far as Indian Society is concerned, radical and revolutionary changes have been taking place over the decades that followed independence. "Political Independence and the progressive growth of industries and commerce brought about many changes in the constitution and alignment of traditional groups like caste and sect, so as to conform to the newly emerging differential distribution pattern of the scarce values of economic power which now included industrial and commercial values in addition to hitherto exclusive economic scarce values of land. As the dynamic elements which initiated these changes have been partly from without and partly from within the society, the resulting changes assumed a non-cumulative character which baffled many of us who tried to interpret them in terms of the integration model of Western functionalists for whom the model has some relavance to the phenomenon of change of West, which unlike the change in our society, is both cumulative as well as in a continuum".[13] Consequently the traditional caste and the sectarian stratification in our society is in a nebulous stage leading to a new pattern of stratification which is yet to be grasped and understood by Indian Sociologists.

As far as Indian Sociology is concerned, the pre-eminent concern was with the phenomenon of caste and sectarian stratification. But such concern has so far failed to penetrate beyond the peripheral and superstructural aspects of stratification, like socio-religious and ritualistic elements. The work of Srinivas[14], Dube[15], Domont[16], Mayer[17], Marriot[18], Lewis[19] and others are of this kind. Though the economic basis, in addition to the super-structural aspects, has been taken into account by a few like Beteille[20], their studies also remain, to a great extent, peripheral in explaining the phenomenon of stratification in a society.

"When we take into consideration the essential features of change in our society particularly its non-cumulative and disintegrative character, an adaptation of dialectical approach

seems to be the most suited one[21] to study the problems of changing pattern of stratification in Indian Society.

2. Dialectical Approach

It was Karl Marx who made a beginning towards dialectical analysis of the phenomenon of stratification. The dialectical approach of Marx involves the analysis of social, cultural, political and other super-structural relations in terms of productive relations.[22] In the sphere of productive relations, he delineated two classes consisting of bourgeoisie who own and control the scarce values and the proletarist who possess only the labour which they undersell to the bourgeoisie. This dichotomous hierarchy extends to all spheres of social relations. The conflicting economic interests ultimately bring about a class struggle, when the expropriated proletariate become conscious of their common economic interest. Thus, the Marxian dialectical approach to startification is founded on the inequitable distribution pattern of the scarce values of social survival in terms of which all super-structural relations in the realm of culture and polity are explained. In other words stratification system is to be analysed in terms of economic system. That is, the meaning of relations in various social and cultural sectors will have to be sought in the conflicting interests of the classes. Thus, in every society the prevalent conflicting economic interests on which stratification system is built up, contain elements of its own change (destruction). This process may continue till an equitable distribution pattern of the scarce value of social survival is achieved.

As against this approach of Marx is the attempt of Max Weber to interpret the phenomenon of stratification in terms of the value system and also by a distinction drawn between three forms of economic, political and social or legal power with corresponding social orders.[23] Though he pointed out that there is reciprocal influence between economic, social and political orders, his main emphasis was on the primacy of value system[24] in determining relations in various spheres. In other words he tried to approach the problem of stratification at the super structural level.

Claiming to be an improvement for the Marxian approach Ralf Dahrendorf[25] has attempted to develop a coercion theory of social stratification. By substituting economic interests by a conception of power, he tried to develop a new conception of class system in which one class is vested with coercive power and hence holds a dominant position while another class is denied of any power and hence occupies a subordinate position. He argued that such forms of stratification are found in social, economic, political and cultural fields and these hierarchical systems need not be interdependent.

Thus, as far as the dialectical approach to social stratification is concerned, systematic studies are yet to be undertaken in indian Sociology. What is attempted here is to approach the problem of stratification from the dialectical angle.

3. Problem of Stratification

During the decades that followed Independence, there has been considerable change in the traditional stratification system in Indian Society. This is particularly true in the former South Travancore region. Till the thirties of this century, the Nadars and Pulayas who constitute the predominant sections in the population of this region were outcastes. After independence, Nadars emerged as a powerful community assuming ownership and control over most of the scarce values of land. At the same time there was little change among pulayas, who even now remain as the agricultural labourers. Before Independence, it was Nairs who constituted the upper caste and upper class in this region. Compared to Nadars and pulayas, the numerical strength of Nairs in the total population was insignificant. But the traditional stratification system enabled them to retain their social and economic dominance till the time of Independence. When the Nadars improved their social, economic and political status, the Nairs came to be relegated to the background. Here it is proposed to study the process which led to various changes in the traditional stratification system in which one section of the outcastes got themselves elevated to upper class position, another section remained static and the traditional upper class got themselves downgraded.

II. CONCEPTS USED FOR THE STUDY

1. Stratification System

For the purpose of the study, a stratification system may be defined as a pattern of ordering of social relations within a society conforming to an inequitable distribution pattern of the scarce values of social survival. Such a stratified system involves hierarchical ordering of economic divisions, a supporting normatibe and value system and the patterns of conformity and non-conformity with a corresponding system of rewards and punishments. Based on the degree of ownership and control over the scarce values of social survival and each group is placed in a hierarchy so that those with the maximum degree of ownership and control occupy the apex, while the wage labourers possessing neither ownership nor control of scarce values occupy the bottom.

2. Inequitable distribution pattern of scarce values of Social Survival

The values which are necessary for man's survival are scarce. among these values, means of production constitute the scarcest and continue to be more and more scarce as time passes and population increases. Closely linked to the scarce values of production are the scarce value of political power which is a social variation of the former.[26] The ownership and control over these values are distributed among various groups in different measures constituting a differential distribution pattern of scarce values.

3. Group

For the purpose of this study, a group is defined as a collectivity of individuals having certain common interests. The numbers are conscious of these common interests which bind them together.[27]

4. Lower Class

Those who are engaged in manual labour either in cultiva-

ting their own land or land belonging to others are classified as lower class for the purpose of this study.

5. Upper Class

Those who own land and live on either the rent from such land or by cultivating such land by employing others without rendering any manual labour by themselves.

6. Middle Class

The concept of middle class is used in this study to represent those who do not resort to manual labour and at the same time possess a monthly income ranging between Rs. 200 and Rs. 300. This categorization is one which is made by the villagers.

III. METHOD

1. Field and Data Collection

The study was carried out in three villages from the former South Travancore region. The villages were selected in such a way that each of them had a predominant population of Nadars, Nairs and Pulayas. Kollal, Vavara and Viakkalloor were the three villages which were thus selected. Kollal is a village which has registered the maximum change in the stratification system. In this villages, Nadars constitute the upper class followed by Nairs and Pulayas. As far as the stratification is concerned, the second village—Vavara—is in a state of transition. Here the traditional Nair upper class compete with the emerging Nadar Upper Class. The third village—Viakkalloor—has been selected to represent the traditional pattern of stratification. Here the Nairs constitute the Upper Class followed by Nadars and Pulayas.

The data were collected by personal observation, case studies, interviewing village leaders and members of Nair. Nadars and Pulayas houseolds, who were selected by the method of random stratified sampling. An interview guide and

TABLE 1

The Total Number of Households and the Selected Sample in these Villages

Castes	*Kollal*		*Vavara*		*Viakkalloor*		*Grand Total*	
	Total	*Selected*	*Total*	*Selected*	*Total*	*Selected*	*Total*	*Selected*
Nairs	43	22	54	27	51	25	148	74
Nadars	110	56	84	43	32	16	228	113
Pulayas	15	7	41	23	61	30	117	60
Total	I08	83	181	93	144	71	493	247

TABLE 2

Class Classification of the Selected Sample in the Three Villages

Class	*Kollal*		*Vavara*		*Viakkalloor*		*Grand Total*	
	Frequency	*Percentage*	*Frequency*	*Percentage*	*Frequency*	*Percentage*	*Frequency*	*Percentage*
Upper	13	15.66	19	20·43	16	22·53	48	19·42
Lower	70	84.34	74	79·57	55	77·47	199	80·58
Total	83	100·00	93	100·00	71	100·00	247	100·00

schedule were prepared on the basis of a preliminary study. A pilot study was conducted and necessary change were made in the schedule in the light of the pilot study. Maximum possible objectivity was maintained throughout. Field work was spread over a period of eleven months.

2. Sampling and Analysis

It was found from the preliminary study that the attitude and behaviour patterns of the adult members of each household regarding stratification do not register significant variation and hence only one adult member from each household was selected for interview. In the three villages, 50 per cent of the house-holds from each caste were selected by the method of random sampling and one adult member from each household was interviewed with the help of an interview schedule. The total number of households from each caste in the selected villages and the number of cases selected for the study are given in Table 1. In Table 2, the class classification of the selected sample is given. In all, two hundred and forty seven (247) cases were selected.

The analysis was carried out on the basis of caste class background of the respondents. For the analysis on the basis of class, the sample population was classified into upper and lower classes on the basis of whether they are engagedin manual labour or not. Those who do not do manual labour and employ others for the same are included under upper class. Those who are engaged in manual labour either in cultivating their own land or land belonging to others are classified as lower class.

NOTES

1. Talcott Parsons, "A Revised Analytical Approach to the Theory of Social Stratification", Essays in Sociological Theory, Glenco : The Free Press, 1954, pp. 386 439.
2. S.N Eisenstadt, Prestiege, participation and Strata Formation", from J.A. Jackson (ed.) Sociological Studies 1–Social Stratification". Cambridge Universiry Press, 1968, p. 72,

3. R. Kornhauser, "The Warner Approach to the Theory of Social Stratification" from Bendix & Lipset (eds.), *Class Status and power : A Reader in Social Stratification*, Glenco : The Free Press, 1962 p. 225.

4. Talcott Parsons, "A Revised Analytical Approach to the theory of Social Stratification" from Bendix & Lipset (eds.) "Class, status and power : A Reader in Social Stratification.', Glenco : The Free Press, 1962,

5. Weoazimierz Wesolowski aud Kazimerz Slowezynski, "Social Stratification in Polish Cities" from J A. Jackson (ed.) "Sociological Studies 1—Social Stratification", Cambridge University Press, 1968, p. 176.

6. Talcott Parsons, "A Revised Analytical Approach to the Theory of Social Stratification", *op. cit.*

7. Kingsley Davis, "Human Society", New York: The Macmillan Co, 1949, pp. 364-391.

8. Wilbert E. Moore, "Social Change", Prentice Hall of India (P) Ltd., New Delhi, 1965.

"Man, Time & Society", John Wiley & Sons., Inc., New York, 1963.

"Order and Change", Essays in Comparative Sociology" John Wiley & Sons., Inc., 1967.

"A Reconsideration of Theories of Social Change", American Sociological Review, 1960, 25, pp. 810-818.

9. Arthur W. Korhanser (ed.) "Problems of Power in American Democracy". Detroit-Wayne State University Press, 1959.

10. Richard Centres, "The Psychology of Social Classes : A Study of Class Consciousness", Princeton University Press. 1949.

11. Talcott Parsons, *op. cit*.

12 Ramachandra Raj, G. "Industrial Conflict in the Context of Conflicts in the Larger system : A Study of Industrial Conflict in Kerala" I.C.S S.R. Project Report, University of Kerala Trivandrum, 1973, p. 4.

13. *Ibid.*, pp. 5-6.

14. M.N. Srinivas, "Religions and Society among the Coorgs of South India", Oxford University Press, London, 1952, "Caste in Modern India and other Essays", Asia Publishing House, New York, 1962.

15. S.C. Dube, "Indian Village", Cornell University Press, New York, 1955.

16. Lewis Dumont and D. Pocock, (Eds), "Contributions to Indian Sociology No. 2", 1958.

17. A C. Mayer, "Caste and Kinship in Central India", Berkeley, University of California Press, 1960.

18. Mckim Marriot, "Caste Ranking and Community Structure in Five Regions of India and Pakistan", Deccan College", Poona, 1953.

19. Oscar Lewis, "Village Life in Northern India", Urbana : University of Illinois Press, 1958.

20. Andre Beteille, "Caste, Class and Power : Changing Pattern of Stratification in a Tanjore Village", Bombay, Oxford University Press 1966.

21. G. Ramachandra Raj Changing pattern of Ca.

22. Karl Marx and Engel Fredricks, "The German Ideology" International Publishers, New York, 1947.

23. Max Weber, "Essays in Sociology", Routlege and Kegan Paul, London, 1947, "Theory of Economic and Social Organization".

24. Max Weber, "Protestant Ethics and the Spirit of Capitalism".

25. Ralf Dahrendorf, "Class and Class Conflict in Industrial Society", Routledge and Kegan Paul, London, 1959.

26. G. Ramachandra Raj, "Industrial Conflict in the Context of Conflict in the Larger System", *op. cit*, p. 13.

27. G Ramchandra Raj, "Functions and Dysfunctions of Social Conflict", Popular Prakashan, Bombay, India, 1974, p. 163.

CHAPTER TWO

GEOGRAPHY, ECOLOGY AND SOCIETY OF KOLLAL, VAVARA AND VIAKKALLOOR VILLAGES

The selected three villages—Kollal, Vavara and Viakkalloor—are situated in the former South Travancore Region. Though this region presently forms part of the Tamil Nadu, historically, culturally, geographically and politically it has been a part of Kerala till recently. The administrative separation of this region from the Kerala State took place only on 1st November, 1956.[1] Therefore the society in this region is more a part of Kerala Society than the Tamil Society with which the region is politically integrated recently.

The land that lies between Arabian Sea and the Western ghats comprising the state of Kerala and the Kanyakumary District of Tamil Nadu is believed to be a land reclaimed from the sea by Lord Parasurama. In order to propitiate his sins, Parasurama is said to have donated the land thus reclaimed to sixty four Namboothiri Brahmin families. It is also said that he "brought representatives of various castes and callings" and introduced "certain new customs which turned the immigrants into a community different from their relatives and friends in the land of their previous occupation".[2]

The Namboothiries, who were the rulers and owners of the land, divided the region into four districts and each district was sub-divided into villages. They became "the Lords of the land in virtue of Parasurama's grant".[3] As the Namboothiries were numerically small, they could not effectively rule the land and hence in A.D. 260, a king was brought down from a neighbouring country to govern Kerala. With this started the Perumal Rule which continued till A.D. 428, when the last Perumal partitioned and bequeathed his country to his kith and kin".[4] From then on Kerala was divided into small principalities and kingdoms. The Venad, which thus emerged, was one such principality which covered the present Kanyakumary District. By the middle of 18th century, Marthanda Varma who was the king of Venad, annexed many kingdoms like Kanyakulam, Ambalapusha and Thekumoor, (1750 AD).[5] He thus, founded the Travancore State which extended from Cape Comerin in South to Cochin in the North. Travancore continued to maintain its separate political entity till Independence. The present Kanyakumary District which is now under the control of Tamil Nadu Government, remained as a part of Travancore-Cochin State till 1956.

Traditional Caste System in South Travancore

The gradation of caste and the rules governing hypergamy, endogamy and exogamy, that are obtained in this region are homologous to those that are prevalent in other parts of Kerala.

Namboothiries used to occupy the highest position in the South Travancore hierarchy of caste system. They were the landlords and owned the Hindu Worshipping centres. But with the collapse of Perumal Rule, they gradually lost economic and political supremacy to the numerically stronger Nairs. They lost most of their proprietory rights over land to the emergent Nair land-lords. At present they constitute, both numerically and economically, an insignificant group. The Namboothiries used to follow Makkathayam (patrilineal inheritance and patrilocal residence). Though joint family system was prevalent till recently among them, it has now yielded place to nuclear families.

Elayads are also Brahmins, though they had only secondary status to the Namboothiries in the caste hierarchy. It is the Elayads who officiate in the funeral rites. They used to follow the Namboothiries in various customs and usages in relation to marriage, inheritance, pollution etc. They are also numerically very insignificant.

Among the Ambalavasies, Marars alone are found in this region. Their traditional occupation was performance of different services at the temples. They used to follow Marumakkathayam (matrilineal inheritance and matrilocal residence). But now there are only very few ambalavasies who follow the traditional occupation. Most of them identify themselves with Nairs. They are also very few in number and are now almost indistinguishable from other Nairs. There are no Kshathriyas in this region.

Nairs form the dominant caste in this region. Till the middle of 19th century they were a martial caste and it was they who formed the militia of the country. After the Perumal Rule, the highest position in the social and political life of the state came to be vested with the ruling Kshatriyas and Nairs. The Nairs were the traditional Naduvashies and Deshavashies having military and administrative control over the areas under them.[6] With the advent of British Rule, Nairs were disarmed and they lost most of their political authority. Nevertheless, they retained their control over the land and remained as landlords and agriculturalists.

After Independence, Nairs gradually lost their economic dominance to the numerically superior Nadars in the region of South Travancore. After the transfer of South Travancore region to Tamil Nadu, this process was accelerated and in all spheres of social, political and economic life, Nadars replaced Nairs as the dominant group.

Though there were a number of sub-castes like Kiriyam, Illum and Swarupi among Nairs, such distinctions and social prestige which used to be attached to them had totally disappeared by the sixties.

The Marumakkathayam system of inheritance and descent and the Joint Family System which used to be prevalent among Nairs have also disappeared after Independence. At present the Nair families are nuclear consisting of father, mother and their children and sometimes the grandparents. Malayalam is the mother tongue of Nairs.

Though there are four intermediary castes between Nairs and polluting castes, only Veluthedans (Washermen) and Vilakkithala Nairs (Barbars) are found in the South Travancore Region. Like Nairs they also used to follow Marumakkathayam. They are numerically very insignificant and most of them identify themselves with the low castes.

Among the polluting castes, Kammalans occupy the highest status. They are divided into endogamous sub-castes of Marayasari (Carpenter), Kallasari (Mason), Musari (Brazier), and Kollan (Blacksmith). Though all of them were of the same status, there was no inter-marriage among them. Marumakkathayam and polyandry are no more prevalent among them after political Independence. Like Nairs they also speak Malayalam.

Nadars form the numerically most dominant caste in South Travancore Region. They constituted 402,555 of the entire Tamil population of 788,455 in the State.[7] Though the Nairs formed 868,411 in the State population they were spread all over the state. At the same time the Nadars population is almost entirely concentrated in the South Travancore Region. This makes them numerically the most dominant caste in the region. They speak both Malayalam and Tamil. After the integration of the region with the Tamil Nadu, Malayalam is gradually falling into disuse among them.

Nadars are believed to be "emigrants from the Northern coast of Ceylon"[8] They used to be "good fighters, hardy and brave".[9] They were Makkathayies and were strictly monogamous. Their hereditary occupation was drawing toddy from palmera palm and making coarse sugar called, jaggery. Though these traditional occupations still persist among most of the

Nadars, there are many among them who have become agriculturists, land owners, and business men. By the thirties of this century they ceased to be a polluting caste and have replaced Nairs as the ruling group.

Among the slave castes only Pulayas are found in this region. They were the traditional agricultural labourers. Most of them still work as agricultural labourers. They follow Makkathayam. Divorce and Widow remarriage are prevalent. Most of the old customs, beliefs and superstitions are prevalent among them. Black magic, belief in ancestral spirit and demons, pollution in severe form etc., are common among Pulayas.[10]

Christianity made its appearance in the South Travancore region only by early 19th century. Christians in this region belong to the London Mission Society which started its prosylitisation activities in 1806.[11] Those who embraced Christianity were Nadars and Pulayas.

Their conversion to Christianity was greatly accelerated when Colonel Munro became the Dewan of Travancore. By 1824 the L.M.S. began its educational activities by establishing a number of English Schools. The Mission which had only two organisational districts in 1820, expanded rapidly and had six districts by 1873. By this time the society was running 237 schools, one college and a Medical Mission.[12] At present the Mission has 1299 Schools, 14 Colleges and 61 Medical Missions.[13] One peculiarity of Nadar Christians of this region is that they follow most of the Hindu customs and usages. The Hindu Nadars and Christian Nadars freely inter-marry.

Both Nairs and Nadars are active in the political sphere. The region covers one parliamentary constituency and four assembly constituencies. Before 1956, Congress and Communist Party were the only political parties having any sizeable following in the region. But after the integration of the region with the Tamil Nadu, Dravida Munnetra Kazhakam extended its activities to this region also. At present the main political parties to this region are organization Congress,

Dravida Munnetra Kazhakam and the Anna Dravida Munnetra Kazhakam. The Communist Party has lost its influence.

The region has a highly developed communication system with a net work of roads.

THE THREE VILLAGES

Kollal

The Kollal Village covers an area of 1208 acres including cultivable fields surrounding the village. It is boarded on the Northern side by the Manked-Viruvilla Road and by the Thamaravaruni River on the Southern side. On the Western side is a canal which brings water for irrigation from Neyar Dam. On the Eastern side of the village is a small katcha road which links the village with puthukada which is a small township situated about eight kilometers on the Eastern side of the village The Manked-Viruvilla Road links the village with Kuzhithura town which is a marketing centre. The village has a Post-office, an Ayurvedic Hospital, three Hindu Temples, two Churches and a Government Middle School, panchayat Office is also located here.

The coconut and palmera gardens and paddy fields owned by the villagers are located on the Northern, Western and Eastern sides. Cocoanuts, palmera, paddy and betel leaves are the main cultivation in the area.

Nairs, Nadars and Pulayas form the dominant castes in the village. There are 43 Nair families, 110 Nadar families and 15 Pulaya families. There are 5 families of artisan castes (2 Asaries, 2 Blacksmiths and 1 Goldsmith) and 1 family of Vilakkithala Nair (Barbar) (See Table 9). The Nairs who were the traditional land-lords live in the North Western Section of the Village. The Nadars live by the river side on the South-Eastern Section. Pulayas, Artisans and the Barbars live on the Western side along the Canal.

Though the Nairs were landlords and agriculturists, they

lost ownership over most of their land to the newly affluent Nadars of the village. The Nadars who used to work as labourers in the land of Nairs, have considerably improved their economic status. Many of them have become agriculturists and traders. Till the time of Independence it was the Nairs who constituted the most dominant political force. But, in the fifties, the numerically dominant Nadars replaced them. As far as the Pulayas are concerned there has been very little change in their economic and political life. Originally they were attached to Nair landlords and now with the rise of Nadars as land proprietors, many Pulayas have switched their allegiance to them. Apart from this shift in their servile attachment, there has been very little change in the status of Pulayas in the village.

Nadars gradually improved their status and with the conversion of a large number of them to Christianity, they could get English Education also. Now both Nairs and Nadars are eager to educate their children. For the high school education they have to go to Viakkalloor Village or Puthukada which are located on either side of the village. For College Education they used to go either to Trivandrum or Nagercoil. Now with the establishment of a College at Kuzhithura many go there for Collegiate Education. The Pulayas are yet to realize the importance of education. Inspite of various incentives, they do not send their children for education beyond the primary level.

Nairs lost their political influence with the rise of Nadars as an economic and political force. The present panchayat Member of this village is a Nadar who belongs to the D.M.K.

The Nadars and Nairs form two well-organized caste groups in this village. At present it is the Nadars who constitute the dominant group. A section of Pulayas usually take the side of Nairs against Nadars. This is probably due to the traditional slave-master allegiance which existed between Pulayas and Nairs.

The Nadars outnumber all other castes in the village. As they constitute 66.59 per cent of the total population in the

village, they emerged as the most dominant political group after Independence.[14] As the Nairs form only 19.30 per cent, they ceased to exercise any significant political influence after the introduction of adult franchise. Pulayas constitute the weakest section forming only 10.16 per cent of the population. They occupy the lowest position in economic, social and political fields.

There are only two political groups in the village. They are the D.M.K. and the Organization Congress. Till early sixties, the agriculturists and land-lords among Nairs and Nadars used to support the Congress while agricultural labourers among the Nadars and Pulayas used to be with the D.M.K. When the D.M.K. came to be voted into power in 1967, the loyalty of the villagers have undergone considerable change. The upper class consisting of agriculturists, peasants and traders among both Nadars and Nairs have shifted their allegiance to the ruling D.M.K., while a section of the low class among both the castes and the Pulayas supported the Organization Congress.

Vavara

The Vavara Village covers an area of 1860 acres. It lies on the side of Manked-Viruvilla Road. This road links the village with Kuzhithura which is 18 kms. on the Eastern side. On the Eastern side of the village is the Kuzhithura-Manked Road. On the Northern side is the Kuzhithura-Nadakkavoor Road. The wet lands are on the Western side of the village. The main cultivation is paddy. The village is easily accessible by bus. There are three temples and one Church. There is also a Post-Office, Village Office, an Ayurvedic Dispensary, an Allopathic Hospital and one High School.

In this village also Nairs, Nadars and Pulayas form the major caste groups. Though the Nadars are numerically dominating constituting 48 per cent of the population, in economic and political spheres, Nairs are also equally dominant. This is inspite of the fact that they form only 24.80 per cent of the population. Though Nairs were the traditional landlords who used to own the entire land wealth of the village, some of them

lost their land to Nadar tenants. It is because of this that a section of Nadars also could emerge as an equally powerful upper class. When there were no agriculturists among Nadars before fourties, quite a sizable section among them have emerged as agriculturists since then. It was hitherto tenants who became agriculturists. Simultaneously quite a sizable section among Nairs were reduced to the status of peasants and agricultural labourers. Though the Pulayas form 24.98 per cent of the population, they are yet to constitute a significant force in social, economic and political spheres. All of them remain as agricultural wage labour. Apart from these three major castes there are four families belonging to the artisan castes. They include in Asari family, two Blacksmith families and a family of Barbar.

This village also forms part of Arudesha Panchayat. The Panchayat representative from this village is a Nadar. He belongs to the Upper Class Section among the Nadars.

In this Village also caste divisions synchronize with residential segregation. The Nairs live on the Eastern side of the village. The residential location of Nadars is on the Northern side. Pulayas live on the western side near the canals.

Viakkalloor

The Viakkallor Village is located on the sea-shore. It covers an area of 2750 acres. The river Thamravarni flows along the Southern side. On the Eastern side is the canal which links the village with Kollal. On the Northern side is the Kanjampuram Paruthikadavu Road which links the village with Kuzhivila-Viruvilla Road. The village is accessible by country boats as well as by walking. Road Transport does not touch this village. One has to walk four furlongs from Kuzhivila-Viruvilla Road along Kanjampuram-Paruthikadavu Road for reaching the village.

Cocoanut, paddy and betel leaves are the main cultivation in this area. The paddy fields surround the village on the three sides.

The Nairs who almost exclusively own the entire land live on the western and Northern sides. The Nadars live ón the Eastern side and the Pulayas live on the Southern side near the river.

There are four Hindu temples and a Church in the Village. There is also a High School and a Post Office.

Though the Pulayas form 41.03 per cent of the total population, all of them remain as agricultural wage labour. They are almost exclusively dependent on Nair agriculturists in the economic, social and political spheres. All the agriculturists in the village are Nairs. They own almost the entire cultivable land. Though they constitute only 32.60 per cent of the total population, it is they who control all the economic, social and political activities. Like the Pulayas, Nadars in this village are also agricultural wage labour. Excepting three peasant families among the Nadars, none among them own any land. The artisan families in the village include three Asari families, two Blacksmith families, one family of Goldsmith and a family of Barbar. They are also economically dependent on the Nair agriculturists.

The D.M.K. and the Organization Congress are the only political parties operating in this village. Most of the Upper Class Nairs and a small section among Nadars and a sizable section among Pulayas belong to D.M.K. Majority among Nadars and a small section among Pulayas belong to the Organization Congress. The Panchayat member who represents the village is a Nair landlord who belongs to the D.M.K.

It may be pointed out that the Upper Class Nairs and a section of Nadars who now support D.M.K. used to belong to Congress till 1967. They shifted their party allegiance to D.M.K., when it came to power in 1967.

NOTES

1. As a consequence of State Reorganisation Act of 1956 Tamil Nadu lost two districts and a new district called Kanyakumari was added to Tamil Nadu by detaching Thovala, Kalkulam, Agastheeswaram and Vilavancode Taluks of Trivandrum District of Travancore-Cochin State.

2. T.K. Velu Pillai, "Travancore State Manual", Vol. II, The Government of Travancore, 1940, p. 3.

3. *Ibid.*, p. 4.

4. *Ibid.*, pp. 3-6.

5. Achutha Menon, C. "Cochin State Manual", Cochin, Government Press, Ernakulam, 1911, p. 116.

6. G. Ramachandra Raj, "Functions and Dysfunctions of Social Conflict", Popular Prakashan, Bombay, 1974, p. 18.

7. T.K. Velu Pillai, "Travancore State Manual", Vol. I, *op. cit.*, p. 435.

8. Robert Caldwell, "The Tinnevelly Shaman : A Sketch of their religion and their moral condition and characteristics as a caste", Madras, Christian Knowledge Society Press, 1949,

9. T.K. Velu Pillai, "Travancore State Manual", Vol, I, *op. cit.*, p. 856.

10. L.K. Ananthakrishna Aiyar, "The Cochin Tribes and Castes", Vol. I, Cochin. 1909.

11. T.K. Velu Pillai, "Travancore State Manual", Vol. I, *op. cit.*, 1940, p 770.

12. *Ibid.*, Vol. I, pp. 773-774.

13. Church of South India Silver Jubilee Souvenir, South Kerala Diocese, p. 11, 1972.

14. Data for all the three villages were collected from the respective Panchayat Offices.

Chapter Three

CASTE STRATIFICATION

The institution of caste is an exclusive characteristic of the Indian Society.[1] In the traditional Indian Society, caste provided the framework for all human activities.[2] Inspite of great changes that have occurred after political Independence, caste continues to play an important role even today.

In the traditional Indian society, social stratification was essentially caste stratification. The characteristic of stratification like exclusiveness, inclusiveness and the hierarchical relations between the units used to be maintained through the caste system viz., endogamy, hierarchy, restrictions on choice of occupation, civil and religious disabilities and privileges of certain groups and untouchability.[3]

Each caste used to safeguard its inclusive characteristics, interests and positions. Inclusiveness of the caste was maintained by confining membership only to the descendants functioning at any point in time. The hierarchial relations between various castes used to be strictly maintained through various social distance practices like untouchability so that there could be practically no challenge or threat to the positions of various castes in the socio-economic hierarchy. The exclusiveness, inclusiveness and the hierarchical relations are reinforced and strengthened through endogamy, commensality, pollution, purity and specialization of tasks.

Under the traditional caste stratification, the caste is at the apex of the hierarchy, had more or less a near monopoly over the scarce values of land. In other words we can say that the traditional caste system used to synchronize with the differential distribution pattern of scarce values. It may be possible to infer that endogamy, commensality, pollution, purity and specialization of social tasks were essentially for maintaining the differential distribution pattern of scarce values and thereby to perpetuate the upper caste domination.

Religion and Traditional Caste System in the Region

Till the beginning of this century majority of the people and the ruling families in Kerala were Hindus. The other religious sects were Muslims and Jews who constituted only an insignificant few. They were concentrated mostly in a few pockets in Malabar, Cochin and Central Travancore. Former South Travancore was essentially a Hindu region.[4]

As far as the South Travancore Region was concerned, the population was almost exclusively Hindus by religion till 1806, when the London Mission Society was established "to attempt pryselytisation in Travancore".[5] The prominant features of Hindu faith that provided the foundation for traditional caste system in South Travancore were :

1. Belief in transmigration.
2. Substantial Conformity with the rules regarding caste system.
3. Faith in Hindu trinity and the Avatharas and,
4. Faith in Vedas.[6]

The traditional caste system which was prevalent in South Travancore Region was homologous to the one that was prevalent in other parts of Kerala Coast. Though the Namboothiri Brahmins were considered to be the highest caste, they constituted only an insignificant section comprising only a few families. Though these few Namboothiri Brahmins were landlords, they did not possess much social and political influence particularly after the middle of 17th century. Though

the ruling Venad Royal Family (later Travancore) and their few relatives claim to be Kahathriyas, various customs and usages that were prevalent among them and their marital relationship with Nair families show that the Kahathriyas in this region are not in any way different from Nairs excepting that they used to hold political power.[7]

The political and economic power in this region used to be vested on Nairs They were the traditional land-lords owing the entire scarce value of land. Also they were the Naduvazhies and Deshavazhies.[8] Their political and economic power was so supreme that they even almost succeeded in replacing the ruling Rajah with another Nair chieftain who was a relative of the King.[9] In fact the ruling Rajahs had to abide by the dictates of the Deshavazhies and Naduvazhies.

Traditional Caste System in the Three Villages

Nairs, Nadars and Pulayas constitute the major caste groups in the three villages. Though there are a few belonging to the artisan castes, they form only a very insignificant section constituting only 3.5 per cent in Kollal village, 2.22 per cent in Vavara village and 4.22 per cent in Viakkalloor village.

As in other parts of South Travancore region, it was the Nairs who formed the ruling Chieftains and land lords in the three villages. Under the traditional caste system both Nadars and Pulayas were outcastes and did not possess any land of their own. Though a sizable section of Nadars in Kollal and Vavara Villages embraced Christianity by early fourties, there has been very little change in their customs, practices and in several beliefs.

Caste System in Kollal Village

Nairs were the land-lords here. They possessed the entire scarce values of land. In Kollal villages there were three Nair joint families among whom the land was divided. It was believed that there was originally only one joint family which was split up into three and as such all the three joint families used

to claim descent from a common ancestor. Of this three, one of them owned more than half the land while the rest of the land was owned by the other two Nair families. By the middle of fourties, these joint families were partitioned.

The Head of the wealthiest of joint family which owned more than half the land of the village, used to function as the village chief. This family used to run a 'Kalari'.[10] All the three families jointly owned the village temple. The entry in the temple used to be the exclusive preserve of the members of these three families. Even after the temple entry proclamation of 1937, Nadars, Pulayas were not permitted to enter the temple till the time of political Independence.

The Nairs in Kollal village were endogamous and marital relationship were more or less confined to these three families themselves. Cross-Cousin marriages were quite common. Nadars were next to Nairs in the caste hierarchy. Nadars form the majority of the population They were untouchables and their social disabilities disappeared only by the time of political Independence. Nadars were patrilenial and patriarchal.

As social distance practices used to be strictly observed by the upper caste Nairs, Nadars had to keep social and physical distance with them. There was also residential segregation and as a result of this Nadar residences used to be clustered by the river side on the South Eastern Section of the Village. The North Western Section of the village was an exclusive preserve of Nairs. Nadars, on their turn, used to observe pollution against Pulayas who were considered to be inferior to them in the caste hierarchy. The social and cultural activities were confined to their own caste group. As they did not have access to temples owned by Nairs, they established two worshipping centres of their own. They themselves used to perform the priestly functions. There was one Nadar family in the village, whose chief activities were these priestly functions. Apart from these two temples which they have established, two churches were also built by the end of fourties when a large number of Nadars embraced Christianity.

Till the fourties, Nadars were almost exclusively agricultural workers. The only exception were five Nadar families who used to help the Nair landlords for the cultivation of land. As there were only three Nair Joint Families constituting only a few in the total population of the village, it was necessary for them to have a few intermediaries for looking after the cultivation of land. As a result of this the richest Nair family and another Nair family in the village had two Nadar families each to superwise the agricultural operations. Likewise the third Nair family also had one Nadar family to look after the agricultural operations. It was the function of these Nadar supervisors to decide how many Nadar and Pulaya labourers would be required each day for working the lands. The remuneration given to them were much higher compared to other agricultural workers. Also the Nair landlords gave them rent-free houses and land. By the end of thirties these five families became comparatively affluent making it possible for them to undertake agricultural operation on their own in lands which they could secure on lease from Nair land-lords. Apart from these five families there were two other Nadar families who were petty traders in the village As there was little competition and as they had Nair patronage also, they, by early fourties, became almost as affluent as the other five Nadar families. When the Nair families were partitioned by fourties, these affluent Nadars could buy up lands from those Nairs who, on securing ownership and control over their share of land, all of a sudden found it difficult to cultivate such land, Quite a few among them sold out their share. Many others leased out the land to Nadars who were only too willing to become tenants. Thus the number of affluent agriculturists and farmers among the Nadars started increasing rapidly since fourties. At the same time, with the loss of ownership and control over the land, the Nairs gradually became pauperised.

There were three families among the Nadars who were today tappers and there was one family which was engaged in making jaggery. The rest of the Nadars in the village were agricultural workers.

The Pulayas used to be placed at the bottom of the tradi-

tional caste hierarchy. They had only the status of semi-slaves and they were literally owned and controlled by the Nair landlords. There used to be three different sections among Pulaya population and each section used to owe allegiance to one of the three joint-families.

The Pulayas were exclusively agricultural workers. As they were in perpetual bondage to their Nair masters, it was the duty of the respective Nair families to provide for the Pulaya 'Adiyans'[11] under them. They never used to receive any wage and instead the Nair lords used to provide paddy, clothing and other item which were just enough for them to lead, a hand to mouth existence. Even at a late as middle of fifties the Pulayas used to receive wage in kind.

The Pulayas were the worst sufferers of untouchability. They had to keep physical, social and cultural distance with both Nairs and Nadars. They did not even possess the freedom to use public lanes. Residential segregation used to be strictly enforced. Along with artisans and barbars, the Pulayas residences are located on the Western side beyond the canal.

The Pulayas were both patrilenial and patrilocal. Though they were Hindus and most of them are even now Hindus, there is very little in common between Nairs and Pulayas. Their religion was a crude form of Hinduism with a prominance of totemism. They used to worship localised personal gods. They were highly superstitions with a firm faith in black magic.

As far as Kollal village is concerned, the Pulayas form only a very small section of the population. Even in the traditional society, majority of agricultural workers were Nadars. There are only 15 Pulaya families and together they account for only 10.86 per cent of the population though they used to owe allegiance to three Nair Joint Families, after political Independence, they are no more attached to them. At present all of them are attached to the four major agriculturists among the Nadars.

Caste System In Vavara Village

In this village the major caste groups are the Nairs, Nadars

and Pulayas. Apart from the Nairs, Nadars and Pulayas there are only four families of artisans and barbar castes whose number being only 2.2 per cent of the total population which is very insignificant. Under the traditional caste system, Nairs formed the highest caste followed by Nadars and Pulayas.

As in other villages, Nairs in the village were traditional land-lords. Till the middle of fourties there were five Nair Joint Families in the village. Of these five families, three of them had kinship relationship claiming common descent. The other two also had kinship relation with each other having a common ancestor It is believed that originally there were only two joint families of which one was split into three and the other into two. It is also believed that the ancestors of these two families were migrants from North Travancore who came to and settled in the village when they received a land grant from Marthanda Varma who was the first Travancore Rajah. Whatever may be the conjunctures regarding the past, it was these two families who used to own more than half of the cultivable land in the village. The rest used to be shared by the other three families. In any case, till the early thirties, the exclusive ownership over the land was with the Nairs. These families were partitioned by early fourties and with the partition nearly half of their land property passed on to Nadars. Also majority of the Nairs who belonged to the three less affluent Nair Joint Families were reduced to the status of agricultural labour when they alienated their land properties in the course of two decades following the partition of these families. The agriculturists among the Nairs in Vavara Village are the ones who originally belonged to the two affluent Nair families.

There are two temples in the village of which one was jointly owned by two families and the other by the three families. The entry to these temples were strictly limited to Nairs alone. Though the temple, owned by the three families was thrown open to Nadars and Pulayas by the time of political Independence, the other temple which belonged to the two affluent families is still kept as an exclusive family preserve. Only those Nairs who claim descent from these two

families has access to this temple.

Untouchability in a severe form used to be practised in this village also. The Nairs, being the highest caste and the land proprietors, used to keep both Nadars and Pulayas at a physical and social distance. When quite a few Nadars embraced Christianity by the middle of fourties the severity of untouchability came down as far as Nadars were concerned. But for Pulayas this continued till early fifties.

The family of the village Chief used to maintain a 'Kalari' where Nair youths from all the five joint families were imparted training in the use of arms. As Nairs alone could wear arms, it was not difficult for the Nair families in the village to keep the numerically stronger Nadars and Pulayas in subservient positions.

After Nairs, next in the caste hierarchy, came the Nadars. Though they were untouchables and agricultural wage labour like Pulayas, they used to enjoy a slightly higher status. Also they had access to public lanes and they were required to keep only a small physical distance with the Nairs. This is probably because some of them used to be employed as a kind of labour supervisors by the Nair land-lords thereby acquiring a higher status compared to other agricultural workers.

Till the thirties there were six Nadar families who used to supervise the agricultural work on behalf of Nair land-lords. The family of the village chief had two such Nadar families for supervising the agricultural operations. The other four Nair families had one Nadar family each for such work. All these six Nadar families had rent-free land leased to them by their respective Nair land-lords. They also had their own houses provided by the land-lords. As these Nadars could cultivate on their own in the land assigned to them and the remuneration which they used to receive for the supervisory work was relatively much higher than the ones that were given to agricultural workers, these families became comparatively affluent by the thirties. When the joint families were partitioned in

early fourties these Nadars could secure large tracts of land for cultivation on a rental basis. With the land legislation in fifties they literally acquired the ownership over the land, thus leased to them.

Among the Nadars there were three petty shop-keepers also. They also, in course of time, became affluent enabling them to buy land from Nairs after the partition of joint families. Over and above these nine Nadar families a few of hitherto Nadar agricultural workers also could become tenants after the partition of joint families.

In this village also there was residential segregation. The Nairs live on the eastern side of the village near the Mankad-Viruvilla Road. The Nadar residences are confined to the Western side near the wet lands.

As Nadars did not have access to Hindu temples, they had a separate temple of their own where Poojas and rituals used to be performed by one of the Nadar families. When a few Nadars embraced Christianity in the fourties, a church was also built.

The Pulayas used to occupy the lowest position in the caste hierarchy. All of them were agricultural workers and they continue to be so even now. As in other villages here also they were totally dependant on the Nair landlords and had only the status of semi-slaves. There were five groups of families among the Pulayas with each group attached to one of the Nair Joint Families. Majority of them even now continue to be attached to Nair agriculturists while the rest have shifted their allegiance to Nadar agriculturists. Apart from this shift in the allegiance there has been practically no change in the socio-economic life pattern of the Pulayas.

Caste System in Viakkalloor Village

In the Viakkalloor Village also the major caste groups are Nairs, Nadars and Pulayas.

Nairs were the traditional landlords having ownership over the entire land wealth of the village. There were only two joint families of which one of them used to own nearly three fourth of the land. It was the Head of this family who was the village Chief. As the village is not easily accessible, the political power of the village chieftain was supreme. Again it was this family which used to run the 'Kalari' for imparting training in the use of arms to Nair youths. The Nairs in the village had three temples of which two are owned by the chieftain's family and one by the other family. Entry to these temples were strictly confined to Nairs and even now Nadars and Pulayas are not permitted inside. The social distance practices used to be strictly observed by Nairs which enabled them to keep both Nadars and Pulayas effectively in the subordinate and dependent position. Partition of joint family property took place only in late fourties and unlike the other two villages there was practically no alienation of landed properties. As a consequence of this Nairs in this village even now continue to own almost the entire land. As present it is the Nairs who form the agriculturists and middle class peasants in the village. Both Nadars and Pulayas even now continue to be economically and socially not only dependant on Nairs but also in subordinate position.

After Nairs next in the caste hierarchy, were Nadars. Two Nadar families used to be engaged as the labour supervisors to the family of the village chieftain Similarly the other Nair joint family also had one Nadar family to supervise the agricultural operations. As the Nair landlords assigned a few acres of rent free land to these three Nadar families, the status of these three families was relatively higher than the other Nadars of the village. There were two other Nadar families who were petty traders. Excepting these five families among the Nadars all others were agricultural workers. As the Nairs did not alienate the land after the partition of their families, unlike in other villages, Nadars in this village could not register any appreciable improvement in their economic status. Only the five families continued to have middle class status of peasants and petty traders. All others, even after political Independence continue to be agricultural workers.

Though the social distance practices are no more observed, some of the social and physical disabilities of both Nadars and Pulayas exist even now. This is because the Nairs could retain economic dominance, and hence there was little change in the economic subordination of Nadars. There is residential segregation in this village also. The Western and the Eastern sides of the village are exclusively Nair areas. The Nadar residences are confined to the Eastern section of the village. Nadars have one temple in the village. As in other villages one Nadar family attends to various rituals and ceremonies in the temple.

Though the Pulayas constitute numerically the most dominant section of the village population, they are almost totally dependant on Nairs. As in other villages, till recently, they were only semi-slaves attached to two Nair Joint Families. The Pulayas were exclusively agricultural workers. Till the fourties they were not receiving any wage from their Nair landlords. Instead their requirements for a hand to mouth existence used to be provided by their lords. Pulayas were untouchables and they could not move freely within the village nor could they use any public lanes. Only during agricultural seasons, when they had to carry the paddy to the land lords' houses, they could enter the village. Their residences are located outside the village proper on the Southern side near the river bank.

Christianity in South Travancore

Though there are many speculations regarding the arrival of Christians to Kerala Coast, the historical evidences like Copper plates show that Christianity emerged in Kerala only by the 14th century.[12] When the Cochin State became a Vassal of the Portuguese in 1503 A.D. Christianity got a new impetus. As the Portuguese power lasted for about a century and a half, a large number of slave castes in Cochin region embraced Christianity during this period. But the spread of Christianity in Travancore Region began only by early 19th century when Travancore came under the political control of British.

As far as South Travancore Region was concerned the proselitization activities of Christian Missionaries began only in 1806

A.D. when the London Mission Society was established.[13] Colonel Macaulay who was the British resident of Travancore in that year extended both economic and political help to the Mission for its activities. In 1809 the first Church was constructed by the Mission of Mylady with the help of the Resident and the Travancore Government.[14] When Colonel Munroe became the Resident Dewan of Travancore in 1811,[15] the Missionary activities got state patronage and protection. The growth of London Mission Society during this period was phenomenal. In 1840 Colonel Munroe exempted Christians of South Travancore from capitalization tax. He "greatly favoured Mission and used his influence on its behalf."[16]

In 1818 the L.M.S. established its Headquarters at Nagercoil. By this time the Mission secured liberal financial grants in the form of tax free land from the Travancore Government. Also a Missionary of the society was appointed as the Judge of Nagercoil Court by Colonel Munroe. The appointment of a Missionary as a judge enhanced the importance and influence of the Mission considerably. By 1820, the L.M.S. succeeded in converting a sizeable section of the Nadar population of South Travancore. Tamil range of L.M.S. covering the South Travancore Region was divided into two districts with Neyyoor and Nagercoil as their Headquarters. As the royal patronage of the Mission continued till the time of Independence, the society has expanded its activities considerably. The society which started its proselitization activities only in 1806 showed a membership of 1,38,958 in 1931.[17] At present the society which is a constituent of the Church of South India shows the adherents as 14,34,532.[18] By 1940 the Church possessed a Medical Mission at Neyyoor, one College at Nagercoil and 237 Schools in different parts of South Travancore. At present the Mission is running 14 Colleges, 143 Secondary Schools, 1115 Nursery Schools and 21 Technical Schools.[19]

Christian Sects in Selected Villages

Hinduism and Christianity are the dominant religious faiths in the three villages. Till the beginning of this century there were only Hindus in these villages and the proselitization

activities of the L.M.S. Mission were extended to this area only by the twenties. Till the temple entry proclamation of 1937, the Hindu worshipping centres were exclusive preserve of Nairs. Consequently Nadars and Pulayas did not have any access to any of the Hindu Temples. Also untouchability used to be practiced in the most severe form. As a result of this, conversion to Christianity became a short cut for the untouchables to escape from the rigors and handicaps imposed on them by the Hindu caste system. When an untouchable embraced Christianity, he not only escaped from the socio-economic discriminations of the caste system and also at the same time derived social, economic, political and educational benefits accruing through British patronage which used to be extended to the L.M.S. Mission and its adherents.

As the Nadars, compared to Pulayas, were relatively less dependent on their Nair landlords, it was mostly they who embraced Christianity so as to improve their socio-economic status. Among the Nadars there were a few tenants, toddy tappers and petty traders. It was these comparatively affluent section among them who became Christians in the early years.

The Pulayas, who were more or less semi-slaves, could not come out of the influence of Nairs as easily as some of the Nadars. This socio-economic dependence of Pulayas on Nair landlords prevented them from embracing Christianity though they were the worst sufferers under the traditional caste system.

The conversion to Christianity was more in the Kollal and Vavara Villages compared to Viakkalloor Village. In the Kollal village, there was a sizeable section among Nadars who were the tenants of Nair landlords. Also there were quite a few among them who were self-employed as petty-shopkeepers and Jaggery producers. When the L.M.S. extended its activities to the village in early twenties, the Nadar tenants and the self-employed Nadars embraced Christianity. It was mostly agricultural labourers and a negligible few among the self-employed and tenants who remained as Hindus. The conversion of the comparatively affluent among the Nadars to Christianity brought about radical changes in the relations between Nadars and Nairs

in the Kollal Village. The Nadars ceased to be an outcaste and the social and political influence of Nairs over them has considerably diminished.

In the case of Vavara also the tenants and the self-employed among the Nadars embraced Christianity leaving only the agricultural labour among them in the Hindu fold. Here also the Nair landlords lost their social and political controls over the Nadars.

In the Viakkalloor Village the Nadars were mostly agricultural labourers and as such they were as dependent on their Nair landlords as Pulayas. This socio-economic and political dependence prevented the bulk of Nadars in this village from embracing Christianity. There are only two Christian Nadars in this village.

Inspite of the conversion to Christianity, there has been very little difference in the customs and practices between Hindu and Christian Nadars. There are inter-marriages and at present it may be possible to find both Hindus and Christian members in the same family.

Till the thirties, out of a total cultivable land area of 5734 acres, 10 joint families in the three villages together owned 5696 acres Fourteen Nadar families who were the supervisors for agricultural operations under the Nair landlords owned only 58 acres. Excepting these fourteen families, none of the Nadars and Pulayas owned any land in the three villages. Both Pulayas and Nadars were agricultural workers.

There was no tenancy system in the early days and the Nairs used to cultivate the lands directly by employing Nadars and Pulaya workers. The 14 Nadar families used to supervise this work.

The wages were low and that also used to be given in kind rather than cash. At the time of harvest, the Nadar and Pulaya labourers used to be given paddy by which they were to satisfy all their needs throughout the year. If need arises the land

TABLE 3

Ownership of Land in the Three Villages as in 1939

Castes	*Kollal**		*Vavara***		*Viakkalloor****		*Total*	
	No. of Households	*Area in acres*	*No. of Households*	*Area in acres*	*No. of Households*	*Area in acres*	*No. of Households*	*Area in acres*
Nairs	3 (37 50%)	1167 (98.39%)	5 (45.45%)	1811 (98.74%)	2 (40%)	2718 (99.42%)	10 (41.67%)	5696 (98.95%)
Nadars	5 (62.50%)	19 (1.61%)	6 (54 55%)	23 (1.26%)	3 (60%)	16 (0.58%)	14 (58.33%)	58 (1.05%)
Total	8 (100%)	1186 (100%)	11 (100%)	1834 (100%)	5 (100%)	2734 (100%)	24 (100%)	5754 (100%)

* The land records give the ownership details of only 1186 acres of land. The rest were Government lands or unauthorised lands.

** The land records show the ownership details of only 1834 acres of land. The rest were Government lands or unauthorised lands.

*** The land records show only 2724 acres of land. The rest were Government lands or unauthorized lands.

lords used to give paddy and cocoanut during the off seasons also. But they were in the form of loans part of which could be adjusted from their wage during agricultural seasons. Through this arrangement Nadars and other agricultural labourers could lead only a hand to mouth existence, and also they were in perpetual debt to their landlords.

The political power of Nairs and the strict adherence to social distance practices that used to be enforced through such power enabled the Nairs to curb any threat to their economic dominance from both Nadars and Pulayas. For several hundred years this situation continued more or less unaltered and the initial change towards a redistribution of scarce values of land began only by the fourties with the emergence of tenancy system.

The tenancy system which was literally non-existent in the village by early thirties when the joint family were on the eve of disintegration. In Kollal and Vavara villages, the families of Nadar supervisors and some of the families of Nadar traders were given land on lease by the Nair families for undertaking cultivation on their own. In return, these tenants were to give half of the total yield from such lands by way of rent. When the joint families were partitioned by the fourties, many Nairs in Kollal and Vavara villages found it difficult to cultivate the land which they secured through partition. An easy way out for them was to lease out the lands to Nadar tenants. Many hitherto agricultural workers among Nadars also became tenants in this process. But such a tenancy system was more or less confined to Vavara and Kollal villages alone. After political Independence, a number of land legislations were enacted by which fair rents were fixed for lands. Such rents were only nominal and by early sixties, the land thus leased to tenants became their own. The absentee landlordism have been totally abolished.

As a consequence of this, in the place of traditional landlords, there emerged agriculturists. When the Nair landlords became agriculturists and middle class peasants in Viakkalloor village, quite a few among them simultaneously became agricultural workers in Vavara village. As far as Kollal village

TABLE 4

Ownership of Land in the Three Villages as in 1971

Castes	Villages							
	Kollal*		Vavara**		Viakkalloor***		Total	
	No. of households	Area in acres	No. of Households	Area in acres	No. of Households	Area in acres	No. of Households	Area in acres
Nairs	21 (26.25%)	147 (12.53%)	41 (42.28%)	794 (43.55%)	51 (82.26%)	2623 (97.43%)	113 (47.29%)	2564 (54.70%)
Nadars	59 (73.75%)	1026 (87.47%)	56 (57.72%)	1029 (56.45%)	11 (17.74%)	69 (2.57%)	126 (52.71%)	2124 (45.30%)
Total	80 (100%)	1173 (100%)	97 (100%)	1823 (100%)	62 (100%)	2692 (100%)	239 (100%)	4688 (100%)

* The land records give the ownership detail of only 1173 acres. The rest are Government lands or in unauthorised occupation.

** The land records show only 1823 acres of land. The rest are Government lands or under unauthorised occupation.

*** The land record shows only 2692 acres of land. The rest are Government lands or under unauthorised occupation.

is concerned none of the landlords could retain any appreciable tracts of their land and as a result of this they became either middle class peasants or agricultural workers.

On the other hand many Nadar tenants became agriculturists owning vast tracts of land in Kollal village. With the abolition of tenancy system the other tenants of Kollal village became middle class peasants. In Vavara village also a few Nadars became agriculturists and the rest became middle class peasants. In Viakkalloor village, those few Nadar families who were assigned land by Nair landlords became middle class peasants. The trading families among Nadars in all the three villages can also be put under the category of middle class.

Excepting two families in Kollal village, Pulayas in all the three villages continued to be agricultural workers having no ownership over any land.

Caste-System and Pre-Independent Political Administration

Before political Independence, Nairs constituted the ruling class in all the villages. They were the village chieftains and they used to exercise control over Nadars and Pulayas. This political supremacy of Nairs continued till the beginning of fourties and though their political power had a set back after the partition of joint families, they could still retain the political control till the time of Independence.

During fourties when a section of Nadars embraced Christianity in Kollal and Vavara villages, there was a considerable set back in the political authority of Nairs in these two villages. The new converts to Christianity could secure several political privileges, as a consequence to the British patronage that used to be extended to L.M.S Mission.

But by the time of Independence and subsequent to it, when Nairs lost their economic dominance in Kollal and Vavara villages, they simultaneously lost their political influence also,

With the introduction of adult franchise, the numerically dominant section of Nadars in Kollal and Vavara villages could effectively replace the Nairs in the political sphere. But such a situation did not arise in Viakkalloor village where the Nairs continued to retain their economic dominance. As both Nadars and Pulayas continued to be economically dependant on Nair agriculturists and as Nairs were also numerically powerful in this village, the political leadership continued to be vested on them.

Caste System, Traditional Economy and Change

Traditional economy in all the three villages were essentially agricultural. Nairs owned the entire land and agricultural operations used to be carried out with the help of Nadars and Pulayas. But later Nairs lost most of their supremacy in the villages of Vavara and Kollal and Nadars took up their place. In Viakkalloor, there was little change in the economic status of Nairs.

After political Independence, when Nairs rapidly lost their ownership over land, they were forced to be dependant on Nadars in Kollal and Vavara villages. Though both Nadars and Pulayas constituted the agricultural wage labour till the thirties, a section among Nadars emerged as agriculturists and middle class peasants. There was no appreciable change in the economic status of Pulayas.

NOTES

1. Hutton, J.H., "Caste in India", Oxford University Press, 1962.
2. Ghurye, G.S. "Caste, Class and Occupation", Popular Book Depot, 1961.
3. *Ibid.*

   Hutton, J.H. "Caste in India", *op. cit.*

   Dluent E.A.H. "The Caste System in Northern India", Oxford University Press, 1931.

   Ryam B. "Caste in Modern Ceylon", Rugers University, New Jersey, 1953.

   Leach E.R. (Ed.) "Aspects of Caste in South India Ceylon and North West Pakistan", Cambridge University, 1960.

Emile Senart, "Caste in India : The Facts and the System", Methuen & Co., Ltd., London, 1930.

4. T.K. Velu Pillai, "The Travancore State Manual", Vol. I, Government of Travancore, 1940.

5. *Ibid.*, p. 770.

6. *Ibid.*, p. 521.

7. G. Ramachandra Raj, "Functions and Dysfunctions of Social Conflict", Popular Prakashan, Bombay, 1974.

8. Naduvazhies and Desavazhies are the semi-autonomous Political chieftains under the Travancore King.

9. T.K. Velu Pillai, "Travancore State Manual", Vol. I, Government of Travancore, 1940.

10. Kalari was a School where Nair youths used to be trained in the use of arms.

11. Pulayas who were attached to Nair lords used to be called Adiyans.

12. G. Ramachandra Raj "Functions and Dysfunctions of Social Conflict", Popular Prakashan, Bombay, 1974, p. 13.

13. T.K. Velu Pillal, *op. cit.*, Vol. II, p. 770.

14. *Ibid.*

15. *Ibid.*, p. 506.

16. Reverend S. Mateer, "The Land of Charity", p. 207.

17. T.K. Velu Pillal, *op. cit.*, Vol. II, p. 775.

18. Church of South Indian Silver Jubilee Souvenir, South Kerala Diocese, 1972, p. 17.

19. *Ibid.*, p. 11.

CHAPTER FOUR

INTER-CASTE AND INTRA-CASTE RELATIONS

Though caste possesses some of the characteristics of communities and closed groups, they were interdependent. The relationship among individuals within a caste group and the relationship between the individuals of different caste group differ widely. Though the higher castes are socially separated from the lower castes, the former needed the services of the latter not only in economic pursuits but also in social life.

Caste, as a status group forms a community of social relationships, based on a distinctive style of life associated with the appropriate honorific symbols or values ; caste position is birth ascribed and one segment of this group is bounded by functional inter-linkages (at ritual, economic and occupational levels) with other groups which together form what Baikey calls a "closed organic stratification".[1]

Caste membership and status were always ascribed and never achieved. In the traditional society, a person who was born into a particular caste remained in it till his death. "In the caste cultural pattern neither personal qualities nor achievements nor wealth, give any individual an entry to social status which is determined solely by heredity...A fixed hierarchy of dominance and subordination operating on the basis of social segregation and distance, which nourishes generally a striking

disparity of wealth and culture among the social strata distinguishes the caste system".[2]

Occupation was the underlying factor which distinguished the various caste strata. All occupations which had status and power went to the upper castes and the menial jobs went to the lower castes.

While inter-caste relations were primarily economic in nature, intra-caste relations were not only economic but also social and cultural. Social distance practices were practised both by lower as well as by upper caste In the traditional society all social and cultural activities were confined to ones own caste group. "The traditions and limited goals and the social status and occupation of the caste shape, his attitudes towards himself as a caste man and his relative attitudes and behaviour towards the men of the other castes. Thus what one encounters is a 'caste personality' shared in large measure with all the persons belonging to the same or similar caste in the social hierarchy."[3]

Inter-Caste and Intra-Caste Relations in the Selected Villages

As already stated Nairs constituted the highest caste in the three villages. Both Nadars and Pulayas were out castes and were economically dependant on the Nair landlords. Untouchability characterised the inter-caste relations in the villages. The Pulayas were to keep a physical distance with Nairs, and except at the time of agricultural operations, there was practically no contact between Nairs and Pulayas. But untouchability in the case of Nadars were not so severe. The physical distance which they had to keep with Nairs was only nominal. Though there was no social inter-course between Nairs and Nadars the economic interaction between the two castes was more frequent. Moreover there were many Nadars in all the three villages who were assisting the Nair landlords in agricultural operations. This provided them with more prestige and higher status than Pulayas who were only agricultural labourers. Also there were

a few Nadars like the petty traders who were not economically dependant on Nairs.

As the traditional caste hierarchy and the supporting belief and value systems effectively safeguarded the landed interests of Nairs against any threat from Nadars and Pulayas, intra-group rivalries and conflicts were common among Nairs. These rivalries could be found in economic, social and political life of Nairs. Nadars were well organized in economic, social and political activities and there existed mutual co-operation.

But the social, economic and political life of Pulayas were dependant on Nair landlords. They had very little caste solidarity and they had to abide by the dictates of Nair landlords.

Changing Patterns of Inter-Caste Relations

When the L.M.S. emerged as a powerful force, the traditional relation between Nairs and Nadars broke down. In fact, the growth of the mission is a consequence of the efforts on the part of Nadars to improve their economic, social and political status vis-a-vis Nairs. After political Independence, Nadars who were well organized and numerically superior, could control the ruling Congress. From 1952 onwards, it was Nadars who always represented the constituencies in the region in both Madras and Kerala Assemblies. Their economic status also, has considerably risen when the Nadar tenants could get ownership and control over their rented lands. Also as far as their relations with the Nairs were concerned, they could completely eliminate untouchability. Their educational status also, has gone up when more and more youngsters among them acquired University education. Thus, when the Nadars emerged as a powerful group their relations with Nairs became more and more strained.

Caste Solidarity and Caste Stratification

As already pointed out Nairs in the three villages had an almost exclusive control over the scarce values of land. Along with economic dominance, Nairs had political power by which they

could exercise effective control over the socio-economic and political life of both Nadars and Pulayas. The strict adherence to social distance practices like untouchability kept Nadars and Pulayas not only in subordination but also socially and physically quite far away from Nairs. As a consequence of this, social and cultural activities of Nairs were strictly confined to their own caste groups.

The economic monopoly of Nairs which was sanctified through traditional caste system effectively eliminated all kinds of threat and competition for Nairs from both Nadars and Pulayas. Being the sole proprietors of land and as there were no threats from the Nadar and Pulaya outcastes, whatever form of economic competition that existed, were among themselves.

Kollal Village

In Kollal Village through, all the three joint families were supposed to be related by blood, there was a considerable amount of rivalries between these families. The village chiefs' family owned more than half the land in village and hence was the richest among the three. The other two families whose landholdings were comparatively less, had been trying their best to acquire more land either from chieftain's family itself or from neighbouring villages.

The chieftain's family on their turn had been trying to acquire control over more and more land. This situation in the village resulted several times into forcible occupation of land leading to physical assaults. An interesting aspect of such disputes was that whenever the chieftain's family came into conflict with another Nair family, the third family either remained neutral or always sided the chieftain's family. Again when physical confrontation takes place during such disputes, Nadars and Pulayas attached to each family also used to be brought in. But their participation was more forced rather than voluntary and as such as the enmity between two Nair groups never percolated down to Nadars and Pulayas. As far as the Nadar and Pulaya participants were concerned, the hostilities used to cease immediately after such confrontation.

Thus it may be said that when a group has monopoly over the scarce values of production leaving all other groups economically dependant on them and when such monopoly has been sanctified through religion, beliefs and value system then there tends to be very little or practically no economic competition or rivalry between the economically dominant groups and others. On the other hand economic rivalry or competition tends to take place among members of one's own group having monopoly over scarce values. Those having the largest share of scarce value, tend to have maximum support and following from other members within the group. Also political power tends to be vested on those having the largest share of scarce values.

The economic rivalry among the Nairs found its expression not only in economic activities but also in social life as well. As Nadars and Pulayas were kept at a distance without any social and cultural interaction, the social life of Nairs was exclusively confined to their caste alone. But the rivalries between the joint families used to manifest themselves in the social functions like marriage, death etc. The rival families were usually excluded.

In short, the solidarity among Nairs was minimal before the partition of joint families. It came down still further when the joint families were partitioned. The rivalries continued unabated among the members of joint families after the partition in fourties. Though a number of nulear families emerged and there used to be close inter-relation between the members of these joint families, old rivalries and antagonisms persisted between the three groups of nuclear families in the village. The situation continued till the end of fifties by which time the Nairs, almost totally lost their monopoly over land.

Once the Nairs were pauperized and they were reduced from traditional upper class position to the status of middle class peasants and agricultural workers, there gradually emerged an awareness for the necessity to stand united for safeguarding their economic interests

The integration of the region with Tamil Nadu resulted into a near total elimination of whatever political influence which they had even after their loss of economic domination. Since the integration of the region with Tamil Nadu, it took more than a decade for the Nairs to take positive steps to organize themselves into a strong group. It is this emerging anxiety among Nairs to organize themselves into a group off-setting further deterioration of their economic, social and political status that is revealed through the extension of the activities of Nair Service Society in this area. At present Nairs in the village are trying to organize a Nair 'Karayogam' (The village unit of Nair Service Society) under the auspices of Nair Service society.

The Nadars who constituted an intermediary untouchable caste between the upper caste Nairs and untouchable Pulayas, were the traditional agricultural workers in Kollal Village. As the entire land in the village belonged to Nairs, the Nadars were totally dependant on them. The five Nadar families who were assisting the Nair landlords in supervising the agricultural activities and the two Nadar trading families were equally dependant on Nairs. As these seven families had land of their own and had a better income compared to other agricultural labourers, they had a comparatively higher social status than the other Nadars. The leadership of Nadars in the village was vested on these seven families. Though there was acute rivalry among the Nair joint families, there was no such rivalry among the seven comparatively affluent Nadar families. They took the lead in organizing the local Nadar into a well-knit group. Till the partition of joint families the Nadars had to abide by the dictates of the Nair landlords. They were forced to take sides and often had to fight each other while supporting the Nair families. But participation in such Nair rivalries did not create any cleavage among them. Very often they only posed as rivals merely to satisfy their respective landlords.

In social and cultural activities there was close co-operation among the Nadars. In marriage and other functions all of them co-operated with each other.

The high solidarity among the Nadars was not in any way affected even when quite a few among them embraced Christianity. It was these leading seven families among Nadars who initially embraced Christianity and the major motivation for the same was to escape from the caste domination of Nairs. Even this took place after the disintegration of joint families by which time, these seven families became independant of Nair landlords. This was because it was the heads of Nair joint families who assigned land for Nadars and once the families were partitioned individual members or emergent nuclear families could not nullify the assignments. By the end of fourties following these seven families a number of Nadar families also embraced Christianity but the conversion to Christianity did not bring about any change either in the life pattern, belief system or practices. Probably, it was the high degree of solidarity and their common economic interest that prevented any radical reorganization of their life patterns even after conversion to Christianity. Even now it was possible to find both Hindu Nadar as well as Christian Nadars in the same family thereby showing that religious affiliation is the least important factor in the social life of Nadars. In spite of the conversion to Christianity, all of them go by the caste nomenclature rather than by their religious affiliations.

Till the fourties the social and cultural activities were the most crucial ones which promoted solidarity among Nadars. As they could not bargain with Nairs for better wages the only areas where they could stand united were the social and cultural fields. The entire Nadar population of the village used to take active part in organizing festivals in the temples and staging some of the traditional cultural arts. In social functions like marriage, all of them used to come together. Apart from these they had caste panchayat whose members were the Heads of Seven Families who were relatively affluent compared to other Nadars. It was in the caste panchayat that disputes between families used to be settled. There were periodical meetings of caste panchayat and special meetings when disputes arise. Only when the caste panchayat could not settle disputes, they were referred to the village chieftain. But to the knowledge of the present Nadar elders, there was never any occasion for the Nair

Chieftain or other Nairs to interfere with disputes among Nadars.

The solidarity among the Nadars registered a marked increase after the fourties when the Nair joint families were partitioned. As the Nadars were numerically the most dominant in the village and the entire land wealth used to be controlled and owned by the three Nair families, there was a considerable amount of suppressed antagonism towards Nairs. But the Nairs with their economic and political dominance, could effectively curb any kind of opposition from the Nadar population. But the partition of Nair joint families enabled the seven leading Nadar families to acquire more land and also quite a few other Nadar families to elevate themselves to the status of tenants from the position of agricultural workers. This change that had occurred in the fourties made the Nadars to realize that it would be possible for them to give effective economic, political and social competition to the numerically smaller Nairs. When some of them embraced Christianity, they could simultaneously eliminate the caste oppression from the Nairs.

From fourties onwards there was greater solidarity among Nadars in economic and political activities. When the Nairs supported the Travancore Maharajah's rule, Nadars extended their organized support for the freedom movement led by the Congress. This put Nairs and Nadars in opposite political camps resulting in the elimination of the remaining influence which the Nairs had over Nadars. By the time of political Independence the solidarity among Nadars enabled them to take over the political power in the village. For the first time in the history of the village a Nadar was elected as a panchayat member. During this election the Nair contestant could not secure any vote from the Nadars. By the end of fifties, when the region was integrated with Tamil Nadu the Nadars could acquire almost a near total monopoly over land and political power.

But the pauperization of Nairs and the rise of economic and political dominance of Nadars lead to a decrease in the solidarity among Nadars by the sixties. There are thirteen

Nadar families in Kollal village who owned and controlled most of the land. The person who represents the village in the panchayat is the richest among them. There is growing competition between these families for acquiring greater control over land. As a result of this competition which began in fifties, caste panchayat ceased to exist and there are two broad groups among the Nadars of which one is headed by the panchayat member. In organizing temple festivals and also festivals in Church there is often clash between these two groups.

From very early times there were only very few Pulayas in this village. They are attached to Nair landlords. On the basis of their allegiance to respective Nair joint families there were three divisions among Pulayas. They lived in total isolation outside the village and were under the total control of Nair landlords. Though the social and cultural life were confined to their own caste there was practically no solidarity as such among them. They were essentially guided by their allegiance to Nair masters. When the joint families were partitioned in fourties they became no more subservient to Nair landlords. Since then there gradually emerged greater co-operation and solidarity among Pulayas in social and cultural activities. When the Nadars emerged as agriculturists in the village by fifties the Pulayas gradually attached themselves with the leading Nadar agricultural families. There was practically no improvement in their socio-economic life and the land area where they lived outside the village now came to belong to the Nadars. At present they exercise their franchise as directed by the new Nadar Masters. The only difference is that there is greater social and cultural co-operation among them and the earlier divisions among them have disappeared.

Vavara Village

In the Vavara Village also, the monopoly of land used to be vested exclusive on five Nair Joint Families. Though Nadars constituted the dominant section of the population there was practically no threat to the economic dominance to Nairs from the Nadar population. The stringent social distance practices

and the political authority of Nairs kept the Nadars in subordinate position and were effectively prevented from posing even a semblance of protest against Nair economic monopoly.

Though there was no threat to Nair dominance from either Nadars or Pulayas, there was acute rivalries between Nair families in economic sphere and such rivalries transgressed into social and political spheres also.

As the richest two families are supposed to be migrants from North Travancore and as these two families together controlled more than half the total land wealth, the rivalry in the village was between these two families on the one side and the rest of the three families on the other side. The rivalries were mostly over the possession and ownership of land. The three families having the indigenous origin claimed that it was their land that was assigned to the other two families when they came and settled down in the village a century and a half back. On this basis they claimed that the land of these two families rightfully belonged to them and as such any tactics could be used for getting back the land. In the beginning of this century several acres of land belonging to the two richest families were forcibly occupied by other Nairs. Over night huts were built up and Nadar and Pulaya workers attached to them were settled in such huts. As already pointed out, Head of one of these two families was the village chief and majority of Nadar and Pulaya population of the village were economically dependant on them. As soon as these two families came to know about this large scale encroachment they, along with their Nadar and Pulaya supporters, destroyed the huts and evicted the encroachers. Though such large scale encroachment never took place subsequently, there were frequent disputes over various plots of land in different parts of the village. There were also a large number of litigations when both sides approached the courts for enforcing their claim. One of the litigation which disputed the ownership of these two families over their entire land dragged on in the courts for about 75 years and before the court could give a final verdict the families themselves were partitioned and the suit was rejected when individual members of the partitioned families were not prepared to pursue it.

This revalry between the two sections of Nairs in the field of economic activity could be seen in social and political activities also. For various social functions, those belonging to the opposite section of families were never used to be invited, and in conducting marriages, both sides competed with each other to make such functions more and more pompous and lavish.

As each group had its own temple in the village, the festivals in these temples were also occasions for giving expression to the rivalries. Each section tried to celebrate the temple festivals much better than the ones in the other temples.

As the richest two families had comparatively smaller membership compared to the other three families and as they owned bulk of the land they had to be more diligent in managing their land. This was particularly necessary if their rivals were not to take advantage of them. Though they had the assistance from three Nadar families to supervise the agricultural activities, the individual members were also directly involved in supervising agricultural activities. As a consequence of this they were more familiar with agricultural operations compared to the members of the other three families. As far as the other three families were concerned, most of the supervisory work had to be carried out by Nadars and as such there was no direct involvement by them in various agricultural operations. When the families were partitioned in fourties, excepting very few, most of those belonging to these three families were unable to take up cultivation on their own in their respective land shares. It was this situation that necessitated most of them to lease out their lands to their erstwhile Nadar supervisors and also few other Nadar agricultural workers.

As far as the political power of the village was concerned, it was always an exclusive preserve of Nairs particularly the richest two families including the village chief. Very often the three Nair families used to challenge the political authority of the other two families and they often went against the decisions and directions of the village chief. Thus it can be said that solidarity among the upper caste Nairs was minimal till the fourties.

The rivalry between the two sections of Nairs continued for a decade even after the partition of joint families. The large number of nuclear families which emerged out of the partition also aligned broadly into two groups along the same line as before partition.

But during this period majority of those who belonged to the three original joint families had become pauperized when quite a few among them either sold or leased out their land to Nadars. By the middle of fifties, with the land legislations, they literally lost their ownership of their land. Most of them were reduced to the status of agricultural labourers. Only a few could remain as middle class peasants.

Compared to this section of Nairs the other section lost their economic dominance only marginally. Nearly half the nuclear families that emerged out of the richest two Nair families retained their land ownership and continued to carry out cultivation on their own. As far as the rest were concerned, they leased out only part of their land while retaining the bulk with them for direct cultivation. Therefore when land legislations came they sustained only marginal loss of their land. It was because of this that a few descendants of these two families emerged as agriculturists by the end of fifties while the rest became middle class peasants. It can be also seen that there are none among them who are reduced to the status of agricultural labour.

When the Nairs lost their economic and political dominance and the traditional caste system has collaped the intra-group rivalries among Nairs started gradually declining. Though, by the middle of fifties, the rivalries among the Nairs have disappeared, they remained only as an unorganized group without any unity. With the pauperization of the bulk of Nairs the earlier concern for organizing social functions and temple festivals at a large scale almost ceased.

By the sixties the Nairs gradually realized that they must organize themselves into an organized group so as to counter the economic, political and social challenge from Nadars who

by this time have become dominant in all spheres of activities. The attempt to organize Nairs came mostly from the agriculturists among them, who, inspite of their control over quite a substantial amount of land wealth, could not effectively influence the socio-economic and political life of villagers. Though the initial attempts in this direction began in early sixties, it took nearly a decade to bring the Nairs together. A "Karayogam" under the auspices of Nair Service Society was organized in 1971 and under its auspices all the adult Nairs in the village meet once in a month at the house of the Nair agriculturists. The President, Secretaries, Treasurer and the working committee numbers of Karayogam are all rich agriculturists and they are now in a position to control effectively the economic, social and political life of Nairs in the village. The disputes between Nairs are settled by the Karayogam and the advices and the directions of Nair agriculturists are accepted by both the peasants and agricultural workers among them.

As in Kollal Village, in Vavara also, there was little intra-group rivalries among the Nadars. Though they used to take sides with the rival factions among the Nairs, such support used to be strictly confined to the disputes between Nairs themselves. In the social and cultural life, they stood as a united group and the leadership used to be vested on nine Nadar families of whom six were supervisory assistants and three were traders. As the traditional caste system and the social distance practices effectively prevented the Nadars from competing with the Nairs, their joint activities were more or less confined to the social and cultural activites alone. There is also a caste panchayat headed by these nine families and it was the caste panchayat which took the initiative in organizing social and cultural activities. Even minor disputes between Nadars used to be quickly settled through the intervention of caste panchayat and the effective elimination of intra-group rivalries promoted a high degree of social solidarity among them. The periodical assembly of Nadars organized by the Caste Panchayat promoted a high frequency of social interaction and a high degree of social solidarity among them.

The various social functions like marriage were to be organized only in consultation and with the help of caste leaders. They join together in organizing their temple festivals. They were acutely conscious of their higher caste status vis-a-vis the Pulayas and as such all of them were very particular in strictly observing pollution and various social distance practices towards Pulayas.

When the Nair joint families were partitioned in the fourties the six supervisory families and the three trading families were the initial economic beneficiaries when they acquired a large quantum of land by way of lease from Nairs. Very soon a few Nadar labourers also secured land on lease for cultivation. By the middle of fifties when the land legislations were enacted, nearly half the land wealth of the village passed over to the Nadars. By this time the nine families who were the initial beneficiaries of partition became agriculturists owning most of the land which were leased out to them by the Nair landlords.

Though, by the time of Independence, the Nadars partially took over the political dominance by virtue of their numerical strength and ascending economic dominance, they could firmly establish their monopoly over political power only when the region was integrated with Tamil Nadu. Therefore, by early sixties, though the land was more or less evenly divided between Nairs and Nadars, the latter, being well organized and numerically superior, established their near total dominance in the social and political life of the village.

By early sixties there was a split among the Nadar leadership and as a result of this Caste Panchayat became defunct. It was the richest agriculturist among the Nadars who was elected from this village to the panchayat. He is opposed by four Nadar Agriculturists and in this they secured the support of not only a few Nadar peasants but also majority of Nair agriculturists. This rivalry between Nadar agriculturists which began in early sixties has become acute, resulting into a broad division among the Nadar peasants and Nadar workers. At present there are frequent disputes and even litigations,

As in other villages Pulayas of Vavara villages also were semi-slaves. As they were kept at a distance both by Nairs and Nadars and as they were living outside the village, and were not permitted free access inside the village, the social and cultural activities were strictly confined to their own caste. They were living in two sections. All those who were attached to the richest, two Nair families were living in a separate 'Cheri' about a kilometer away from the 'Cheri', where the rest are living. As their status was only that of semi-slaves are their socio-economic and political life were strictly controlled and directed by the Nairs. There was practically no solidarity among them. The various functions and festivals were organized by separate Cheris and the social interactions were more or less confined to the concerned Cheris alone. As their primary allegiance was towards their Nair masters they used to go only to them during crisis and only seldom they sought help among themselves. The lack of education and the lack of opportunity for the same made them to remain in the subordinate position of semi-slaves over hundreds of years and this situation did not undergo much change even after the partition of joint families. Those Pulayas in one of the Cheris owing allegiance to the richest two families continued to be attached to the agriculturists among them after the partition. The Pulayas in the other Cheris shifted their allegiance to the new Nadar agriculturists.

Thus the Pulayas functioned as two groups having little solidarity till the middle of sixties. But starting from late fifties there emerged a new awareness among them as to the necessity for standing united if they were to improve their conditions. By the middle of sixties a few positive steps were taken by the younger elements among them to eliminate the Cheri actionalism. Though a semblance of unity has been now established, they are yet to emerge as a well organized group.

Viakkalloor Village

Unlike other villages Nairs constitute a dominant section of the population in this village. Though at present there are 51 Nair families, originally there were only two large joint families.

The present nuclear families emerged when these two joint families were partitioned.

These two joint families owned all the lands and Head of the richer of the two families was the village chief. The social interaction of Nairs was exclusively confined to their own group. As there was strict adherence to social distance practices like pollution there were practically no cultural contacts between Nairs and other out-castes consisting of Nadars and Pulayas. As this village had a large area of cultivation compared to other villages, these two families brought quite a sizable section of Pulayas from other places for working in the land. It was because of this that the Pulayas are numerically dominant in this village.

As this village chief's family owned nearly three fourth of the land area and as the number of members in this family was comparatively smaller, the economic status of this family was considerably higher than the other family which had a larger membership while owning comparatively smaller area of land. There were frequent disputes between these families over land. But such disputes were always litigational and there was no occasion for any physical confrontation between these families were not cordial yet they used to co-operate with each other in social functions and cultural activities. Inspite of litigations between them whenever there was a function like marriage the members of the other family used to be invited and they used to respond to such invitations. Though each family had their own separate temples, both together used to organize the festivals in each.

The litigations and the mild estrangement between these two families came to an end when the partition of the families took place in late fourties.

An interesting aspect of the agricultural operation that used to be carried out by Nairs in the village was that they used to be directly involved in such operations inspite of the help which they could get from their respective Nadar superiors. It is because of this that when joint families were partitioned, the

Nairs could carry on with the cultivation of their land without leasing them out to Nadar tenants. There were only three cases where part of the land was leased out by Nairs to Nadar tenants. Though partition brought about pauperization of Nairs to certain extent none of them was reduced to the status of agricultural labour. All the agriculturists in the village are the descendants of chieftain's family. The other family, when partitioned lost its economic status considerably. As they had only comparatively smaller area of land while having a large membership, the members of the family were reduced to the status of middle class peasants.

After Independence, when the political influence of Nairs in region as a whole has suffered a slump, it also had its impact on the political influence of Nairs in the village. Till Independence the socio-economic and political life of both Nadars and Pulayas used to be strictly controlled and directed by Nairs. But with the introduction of adult franchise and the emergence of Nadars as a powerful political force in the region, it became difficult for Nairs to exercise the same influence over the local Nadars as before political Independence.

Though intra-group rivalries were not many among the Nairs, they are not a well organized group. During the fifties the three Nair families who leased out part of their land to Nadar tenants, lost such lands to the tenants as a result of land legislations. As similar developments in the neighbouring villages have totally pauperized the erstwhile Nair landlords, the local Nairs also felt that they will have to stand united if the Nadars were not to displace them in the economic, social and political fields. It was a result of this that Nairs began organizing a Karayogam in early sixties and have succeeded in establishing a unit of Nair Service Society by 1970.

After the organization of 'Karayogam' all adult Nairs in the village could meet once in a month to discuss various economic, social and political problems of common interest. At present various social and cultural functions like marriage and temple festivals are arranged through the 'Karayogam'. Every Nair family has to give a monthly donation. Now efforts are being

made to construct a building for Karayogam for which all Nair families of the village have given donations.

The attempt of Nairs to stand united from early sixties and the retention of their monopoly over scarce values have enabled them to retain the traditional dominant position in all sectors of social life in the village. It was because of this that a Nair agriculturist could get elected to the Panchayat. As majority of the Nadars and Pulayas in the village continued to be agricultural workers and hence economically dependant on Nairs, the latter is in a position to influence the socio-economic and political life of Nadars and Pulayas. Excepting five families all other Nadars in the village were agricultural workers. Three of those families who were attached to the two Nair joint families had a few acres of land which were assigned to them by their Nair landlords. Two other families who were running two stores in the village also had a few acres of land. After the partition of joint families three Nairs have given another few acres of land on rent to two Nadar families which later became their own after the enactment of land legislations. At present there are nine middle class peasant families among the Nadars who are the descendants of these five families. All the other Nadars in the village continue to be agricultural workers.

As in other villages Nadars in this village have also a Caste Panchayat headed by the comparatively richer five families. The periodical meetings of the Caste Panchayat enabled the Nadars to come together once in a while thereby promoting a high degree of social interaction among them. There were no intra-group rivalries among them and all disputes between individual families were settled through the Caste Panchayat. After the partition of joint families and particularly after political Independence, the middle class peasants among the Nadars ceased to be any more dependant on Nairs and as such tried to challenge the Nair dominance in the social, economic and political life of the village. During the Panchayat election one of them stood as a candidate and could secure 71 per cent of the Nadar votes. As he could not command any support from Pulayas, he was defeated. Subsequent to this, there were inter-

group rivalries between Nadars and Nairs and as a result of this the solidarity among Nairs marked an increase during sixties. The nine middle class peasant families among Nadars provided the necessary local leadership for the caste members. But this growing competition and rivalries between Nadars and Nairs have adversely affected the economic interest of the agricultural workers among Nadars. At present Nair agriculturists are denying work opportunities for Nadars and the benefit has gone to Pulayas agricultural workers. Most of the local Nadar workers are going out of the village seeking employment while Pulaya workers from other villages were able to secure work in Viakkalloor village. This situation is gradually leading to acute conflicts and the possibility for the eruption of physical violence cannot be ruled out. But at the same time Nadars could achieve a high degree of social cohesion and social solidarity and the intra-group conflicts are totally eliminated.

The Pulayas in this village constitute the most dominant section of the population. But in all spheres of activities they are influenced and directed by the Nair agriculturists.

Majority of the Pulayas were the 'Adidans' of the village chief's family and they continued to be so even now as they are attached to the Nair agriculturists who are the descendants of that family. Though the Pulayas were completely kept out of the main-stream of the socio-economic and political life of the village and were compelled to confine their socio-cultural activities to their own caste, there has been practically no solidarity among them. After Independence, even though social distance practices and social disabilities of Pulayas have disappeared, there has been very little change in their life pattern and belief system. At present, they are making some efforts for getting united as a group so that they can prevent the Nadar agricultural workers from getting employment in the village. Otherwise Pulayas in the village continue to be service to the Nair agriculturists and peasants.

Caste Stratification and Economic Conflict

While the Nadars have considerably improved their economic status, there was no corresponding improvement in the case of Nairs. As they were numerically small, they could not play any crucial role during the post-Independent period. Also land legislations deprived them of their economic superiority. In the field of education and other social activities, they lost their dominance to the numerically dominant Nadars.

In the economic field there is tough competition which leads often to conflict between Nadars and Nairs. Both groups are acutely conscious of their conflicting interests. This conflict is more pronounced in the agricultural sector. In the Kollal village, the Nadars could almost totally replace the Nairs with respect to land holdings. They could assume the ownership and control over almost the entire cultivable land. The erstwhile Nair landlords have been reduced to the status of peasants and agricultural workers. In the Vavara village the scarce value of land is more or less evenly divided between Nair and Nadar agriculturists. In this village economic competition between Nairs and Nadars is extremely acute. In the Viakkalloor village, though Nair agriculturists and peasants could still retain the control over the land, they are facing a tough competition with the well organized Nadar peasants and agricultural workers. Any way in all the three villages both Nairs and Nadars are acutely conscious of their competition in the economic field.

As far as the Pulayas are concerned there has been very little change in the economic, social, political and educational statutes. In Vavara and Kollal villages their traditional economic dependance on Nairs came to be substituted by dependance on the emergent Nadar agriculturists. In other words their economic dependance continues unabated. They are acutely conscious of their economic dependance and most of them feel that they have conflicting economic interests with Nairs and Nadars. But on the other hand neither the Nairs nor the Nadars recognize any such conflicting interest between them and pulayas. This may be because the Pulayas are neither

TABLE 5[4]

Awareness Among Different Caste Groups Regarding Economic Competition

Responses	*Among Nairs & Nadars*		*Among Nadars & Nairs*		*Among Pulayas & Nairs*		*Among Pulayas & Nadars*	
	Frequency	*Percentage*	*Frequency*	*Percentage*	*Frequency*	*Percentage*	*Frequency*	*Percentage*
Competitive	37	50	59	52.22	29	48.34	20	33.33
Conflict	8	10.82	13	11.50	—	—	1	1.67
Cordial	7	9.46	28	24.78	3	5	11	18.34
Indifferent	22	29.72	13	11.50	28	46.66	28	46.66
Total	74	100.00	113	100.00	60	100.00	60	100.00

4. Appendix 1 Q-III 5.

organized nor do they own or control any land. As such, they are not in a position to pose any threat to the economic interests of Nadars and Nairs.

Under the traditional caste hierarchy in the three villages, Nairs being the land owners had the highest economic status followed by Nadar supervisors, petty traders and agricultural workers among the Nadars. The lowest position used to be occupied by pulayas and all of them were agricultural wage labourers. During the course of two decades that followed Independence the economic status of Nairs has undergone considerable deterioration. 72.98 per cent of the Nair respondents and 65.49 per cent of Nadar respondents accepted that their status was considerably deteriorated of the Independance. Many of them have been reduced to agricultural labour in Kollal and Vavara villages and hence many of them came to be dependant on the newly affluent Nadars in these two villages. Partition of joint family properties and mutual rivalries contributed to this economic deterioration of Nadars.

In the case of Nadars there was considerable improvement in their economic status. A considerable section of the sample —91.89 per cent of Nair, 84.96 per cent of Nadars and 86.66% of Pulayas—were ready to accept the improved status of Nadars. Group solidarity and mutual co-operation have contributed to this improvement. Many tenants among them have become land proprietors. Petty businessmen and traders among them also acquired ownership over land.

As far as the Pulayas are concerned, their economic condition remains more or less unchanged. By and large they even now remain as agricultural wage labour.

Though, for majority, caste is not a basis for economic transactions, there is a sizable section whose sectarian orientation is manifested in their economic interactions. Nairs, compared to Nadars, are more sectarian oriented in their economic dealings. There are many among them who confines their economic activities to their own caste group (33.79 per cent).

This may be because, during the years that followed political Independence it was Nadars who always benefitted in various economic transactions between Nairs and Nadars. In this process many Nair land lords were reduced to agriculture wage labour in Vavara and Kollal villages, while the Nadar tenants became land proprietors. It is probably as a consequence to this, that the Nairs are found to be reluctant to have economic transactions with Nadars (1.35 per cent). The Nadars who have been benefiting through the economic interaction with Nairs are found to have economic dealings with Nairs and Pulayas. Moreover, as they were dependant on Nair land lords till recently, they could improve their economic status only through such relations with Nairs. In the case of Pulayas they had no other option but to maintain economic relation with both Nadars and Nairs. As they were agricultural labourers they are dependant on the economically affluent section among Nairs and Nadars.

Caste Stratification and Political Activities

In political activities, till the time of Independence, the Nairs used to constitute the dominant group. They constituted the rulers and the militia. In the case of these three villages also the political leadership used to be vested on Nairs alone. Both Nadars and Pulayas were under the political control of Nairs. Political activities and political rivalries were the exclusive pre-occupation of the affluent Nairs. But, after political Independence, this situation has changed in all the three villagers. With the emergence of Nadars as a powerful economic and political group, Nairs lost their political dominance in Kollal and Vavara villages. As they were numerically weaker compared to Nadars and when they lost their control over the scarce values of land to the newly affluent Nadars, they ceased to have any political influence over most of the Nadars and Pulayas. In the Viakkalloor village the Nairs still retain political control because they continue to constitute the dominant economic group. At the time of Independence most of the Nairs were with the ruling Congress. This made a considerable section among the Nadars and the Pulayas to shift their allegiance to D.M.K. When the Congress lost political control to

D.M.K., the Nairs ceased to have any political influence in these two villages. But, gradually, the upper class section among Nairs left the Congress and joined the D.M.K. Simultaneously the lower class sections among the Nadars and Pulayas left D.M.K. and joined the Congress. At present bulk of the Nairs and the lower class sections among Nadars and Pulayas support Congress while the affluent Nadars and a few among the Nairs who still retain the upper class position support the ruling D.M.K. On the whole the relation between Nairs and Nadars in the political sphere is conflicting (50 per cent). But the relation between Nairs and Pulayas are cordial (51.35 per cent).

With the loss of upper class position the political status of Nairs have deteriorated completely. Those who represent the Kollal and Vavara village in the Panchayat are Nadars who belong to D.M.K. Party. Only the Viakkalloor village where the Nairs retain the upper class positions the representative belongs to the Nair community. On the other hand as in the case of economic status there was considerable improvement in the political status of Nadars. As they are numerically stronger they are able to acquire exclusive political power in Vavara and Kollal villages relegating the hitherto dominant Nairs to subordinate positions. As far as the Pulayas are concerned they did not possess any political status in the early days and the position remain more or less unchanged even now.

Though participation in political activities are to a great extent dependent on economic status yet caste and sectarian feelings are found to have a dominant role in political relations. Irrespective of the economic background, Nairs, Nadars and Pulayas are found to prefer only those who belong to their own caste for the political representation of their constituency and the village (Tables 6 & 7).

For political leadership, caste affiliation was found to play a dominant role. The leadership in each caste is found to be vested on the economically affluent section among them (54.68 per cent). It was found that the Nadars who represent the Vavara and Kollal villages in the Panchayat and the Nairs who represent the Viakkalloor village are from the upper class

TABLE 6

Preference for the Sectarian Background of Panchayat President[5]

Castes	From Nairs	From Nadars	From Pulayas	No Caste Preference	Total
Nairs	30 (40.54%)	2 (2.7%)	—	42 (56.76%)	74 (100%)
Nadars	—	25 (22.12%)	2 (1.78%)	86 (76.10%)	113 (100%)
Pulayas	—	1 (1.67%)	12 (20%)	47 (78.33%)	60 (100%)
Total	30 (12.14%)	28 (11.34%)	14 (6.67%)	175 (70.85%)	247 (100%)

$X^2 = 98.4138$ $X^2.99(6) = 16.81$

Significant at 1% level.

TABLE 7

Sectarian Preference in the Representation of the Constituency[6]

Castes	From Nairs	From Nadars	From Pulayas	No Caste Preference	Total
Nairs	27 (36.50%)	2 (2.70%)	—	45 (60.80%)	74 (100%)
Nadars	—	26 (23.02%)	1 (0.88%)	86 (76.10%)	113 (100%)
Pulayas	—	—	10 (16.66%)	50 (83 34%)	60 (100%)
Total	27 (10.94%)	28 (11.34%)	11 (4 46%)	181 (73.26%)	247 (100%)

$X^2 = 61.9918$ $X^2.99(6) = 16.81$

Significant at 1% level.

section. All three of them are richest agriculturalists in their respective villages. It was found that each caste group considers income as an important factor that determines leadership.

In all Panchayat and Assembly elections, caste affiliations play a dominant role in voting behaviour (70.(4 per cent). In all the three villages, whenever the Nadar candidates were opposed by Nair candidates the voting was never based on political affiliations. The Nairs used to vote enblock for Nair candidates (71.63 per cent) while the Nadars supported their caste candidate (69.03 per cent). Depending on the economic dependence, Pulayas used to divide their votes between Nairs and Nadar candidates. But, when both the candidates belong to the same caste, the voting was based on party affiliations and also on caste affiliations. In such situations, as was the case with the last Panchayat elections, the affluent section among Nairs and Nadars voted for the D.M.K. The votes of the agriculture wage labour among Nairs, Nadars and Pulayas were divided between Congress and D.M.K. This was because the Nair and Nadar agriculturalists persuaded a section of the agriculture wage labour who are economically dependant on them to exercise their franchise in favour of their candidates. Any way it can be said that caste considerations determine the nature of voting during elections and the caste interests are taken into account while a voter exercises his franchise.

There is rivalry between Nairs and Nadars for assuming dominant positions of power in both the major political parties of D.M.K. and Organization Congress. But this rivalry is more or less confined to the richest sections of these two castes and those who are economically dependant on them. As far as the ruling D.M.K. is concerned, all important political positions are occupied by Nadar agriculturalists in Kollal village and evenly divided between Nadars and Nairs in Vavara village. In Viakkalloor village it is the Nairs who occupy important party positions. Excepting a section of Pulayas depending on Nadar landlords most of them extend their support to the Congress Organization. Quite a sizable section among the unskilled Nadar labourers also support the Congress Organization. But, on the whole, the ruling D.M.K. lead by richer sections among Nadar agriculturalists is the politically dominant party in the two villages. In the Viakkalloor village the Nairs constitute the politically dominant section. They are with the D.M K. Bulk of the Pulaya and

Nadar populations of the village are economically dependant on Nair agriculturalists and they extend their support to Nairs in the political field also. Consequently the Panchayat representative of this village is a Nair agriculturalist belonging to D.M.K. The Congress Organization gets support only from a small section of the Nadar and Pulaya agriculture labourers. But the leadership of the Congress Organization in the village is vested on a Nair agriculturalist.

Caste Stratification and Social and Educational Activities

Under the traditional caste system the social life of each caste used to be confined to the respective caste members. The social distance practices like untouchability provided social and physical barrier between various castes. The social interaction among the Nairs in the three villages use to be confined to Nairs alone. They owned the temples in which neither the Nadars nor the Pulayas had any access. The festivals of the temples were exclusively a preserve of Nairs alone. In marriages and various other celebrations and ceremonies organized by the Nairs, no other caste in the village used to be invited. There was no occasion in which there could be any social gathering where Nairs and other castes could freely mingle with each other.

As far as Nadars were concerned they did not have any social interaction neither with the upper caste Nairs nor the Pulayas. But social interaction among them was more frequent and intense than are found either among the Nairs or the Pulayas. Being the tenants of Nairs they used to give donations in kind and cash to their respective land lords at the time of their festivals, marriage ceremonies etc. Apart from such contacts which were more economic in nature rather than social, there were no other interaction between Nadars and the high caste Nairs. Moreover in all the three villages it is possible to see a kind of residential segregation between Nadars and Nairs which prevent free social interaction.

In the case of Pulayas residential segregation was more

marked with their houses located at the periphery of the villages. In the social life they never used to have any contact whatsoever neither with the Nadars nor the Nairs. Their social life was much more isolated than both the other castes. But, being the agricultural wage labour attached to various Nair landlords, the Pulayas had to work in the houses of Nair land lords at the time of important festivals, ceremonies etc. But they always used to be kept at a physical and social distance and could never participate in any of the functions for organizing which they had to provide their labour.

But after political Independence, the situation has considerably changed. The abolition of untouchability and other social distance practices eliminated the traditional socio-cultural barriers between the three castes. But also this did not accelerate the social interaction between the various castes. The major development in the socio-cultural life of the three castes in the villages was the progressive decline of the social status of Nairs and the phenomenal rise in the social status of Nadars. In Kollal village the Nadars have risen so much in their social status that the Nairs have been reduced to subservient positions. Almost all the social and cultural activities in this village are organized and planned by the Nadars. In this the leadership is taken over by the affluent section among them. The Hindu and Christian festivals which the Nadars organize have become the leading and most important ones while the hitherto important festivals of Nairs ceased to be of any significance or importance in the village life. As far as the Pulayas in the village are concerned there has been no appreciable change in their social life. Their festivals and celebrations continue to be ignored by both Nadars and Nairs. Villagers themselves are conscious of this situation in the social life of Pulayas.

In the social and cultural life, there is rivalry between Nairs and Nadars in all the three villages. But, in the early days, the socio-cultural relations between the communities were harmonious and cordial. The Nair land lords in these three villages used to help both Nairs and Nadars in organizing various social and cultural activities by providing patronage

and financial help. But there was no mutual participation in such activities. When the Nadars improved their economic status in Vavara and Kollal villages, the socio-cultural activities of Nairs and Nadars assumed a competitive character. In organizing festival and ceremonies like marriage etc. the affluent among each community tried to surpass the ones organized by others. But in Viakkalloor village the economic status of Nadars did not have any appreciable betterment. Though the social and cultural relations were harmonious and cordial till recently, of late, competitive and conflicting relations are gradually emerging. Pulayas in all the three villages are found to maintain cordial relations with both Nairs and Nadars in the social and cultural activities.

Till a early thirties of this century formal education was almost an exclusive preserve of Nairs. The socio-economic and political privileges which they enjoyed in the early days provided them with exclusive rights in the field of education also. The early form of education prevalent in the three villages was predominantly physical education. The most influential and richest families used to have their own Kalaries (Physical Education Schools) where necessary training in the use of arms used to be imparted to Nair youths. Apart from these there used to be no other formal education. By the beginning of this century, when formal English Education was introduced, Nair continued to maintain their monopoly in English Education also.

In the case of Nadars and Pulayas there were no institutional arrangements for any kind of education. By and large, they remained illiterates. But by the thirties, with the change in the socio-economic status of Nadars, they could progressively acquire English Education. The conversion to Christianity in Kollal and Vavara villages enabled the Nadars to have greater influence in the field of education. As the pioneers in the field of English Education were Christian Missionaries, Nadar Christians came to have better opportunities for getting English Education.

At present, Nadars in Vavara and Kollal villages, compared

to Nairs, have more opportunities for higher education. On the other hand, with the deteriorated socio-economic and political status, Nairs are not in a position to provide adequate education to their youth. In both these villages the competition between these two communities are acute in the field of education. As far as the Viakkalloor village is concerned, Nairs are, even now, better placed to provide formal education to their children. The Nadars in this village are also availing the educational opportunities provided to them by the L.M S. Mission. This is inspite of any appreciable improvement in the socio-economic status of Nadars in this village. The educated Nadar youths in this village are no more subservient to Nairs. This has given rise to potential conflict situations between Nadars and Nairs. But, so far, these conflict situations have not developed into overt physical confrontation between these communities.

As far as the Pulayas in the three villages are concerned, they are yet to make use of educational opportunities available to them. Though their children can get grants and other financial aids from Government there are not many who have acquired formal education. This may be because, in all the three villages, they are totally dependant and subservient to Nadars and Nairs in socio-economic activities.

Changing Patterns of Intra-Caste Relations

Under the traditional caste system social interaction used to be almost exclusively confined to each caste. The economic dependance of Nadars and Pulayas on Nairs were near total and as such, inspite of common interests and common social characteristics of each caste, they seldom functioned as organized groups. When economic and political dominance of Nairs inhibited any challenge or threat to their positions from Nadars and Pulayas, there was no occasion for the latter to have any kind of conflicting relations with the Nair upper-castes. Therefore the conflicts were mostly intra-caste conflicts rather than inter-caste conflicts. This was more marked among the Nairs in the three villages. They, being the upper caste and upper class, did not face any competition or conflict from the lower

castes. This situation prevented the emergence of any kind of caste solidarity among them. Consequently intra-group rivalries and conflicts were frequent and acute among them. The challenge to the economic interests of individual Nairs were exclusively from within the group. This lead to acute intra-group conflict among them in the field of economic activities. These conflicts in the economic field transgressed into social and political life as well. In the case of Nadars and Pulayas also the situation was in no way different. Intra-group conflicts which used to manifest through even violence were rempant in both castes. But by the thirties of this century the situation has considerably changed. The numerically dominant Nadars in Kollal and Vavara village improved their economic status and they gradually posed a challenge to Nair dominance in the economic field. This has led to the emergence of inter-group rivalries and conflicts between Nairs and Nadars. But simultaneously there began emerging caste solidarity and a gradual decline of intra-group conflicts. By the time of political Independence caste solidarity among Nadars has considerably increased. But, at the same time, after political Independence, caste solidarity among the Nairs also began emerging. This was probably because only by the time of political Independence, the Nairs could realise the challenge posed to their positions by the Nadars. The caste solidarity was to emerge only still later among Pulayas. In any case it can be seen that caste solidarity has increased among all the three castes in the three villages.

The traditional caste stratification was essentially an institutional arrangement for legitimising the Nair monopoly over the scarce values of land. Though it was a three-tier-caste stratification that existed in the three villages, in terms of distribution pattern of scarce values, it was a dichotomic division with Nairs owing all the scarce values leaving both Nadars and Pulayas as wage labour. By partially giving ownership over a little land and by assigning supervisory roles to a negligibly few families, the Nadars were given a higher status compared to Pulayas. But, at the same time, their role was essentially that of agriculture labour. But the redistribution of scarce values began with the partition of Nair joint families

and the process was further accelerated after political Independence. When land legislations were enacted. Nadar tenants could acquire ownership over the leased lands. This redistribution of scarce values is followed by the disintegration of the caste system which provided the institutional sanctifications and legistimisations for the land monopoly. With this development, the hierarchial caste system has been replaced by caste groupings leading to the emergence of caste solidarity. But it may be noted that the hierarchial stratification used to synchronize with class stratification till the fourties. But when the caste stratification is replaced by horizontal caste groupings a new pattern of class stratification has emerged which has cut across the caste groupings.

TABLE 8

Caste Solidarity After Political Independence[7]

Castes	*Same as before*	*Increased*	*Decreased*	*Total*
Nairs	17 (22.97%)	47 (63.51%)	10 (13.52%)	74 (100%)
Nadars	71 (62.83%)	22 (19.47%)	20 (17.70%)	113 (100%)
Pulayas	24 (40%)	22 (36 67%)	14 (17.82%)	60 (100%)
Total	112 (45.34%)	91 (36.84%)	44 (17.82%)	247 (100%)
X^2	=10.6144	X^2 .99(4)=13.28	Not Significant at 1% level. Significant at 5% level.	

With the emergence of solidarity among Nairs and the new awareness of Pulayas to stand united have led to the development of greater inter-dependence between the members of the caste. This inter-dependence is found in economic, social, political and educational activities. Though it is class stratification rather than caste stratification that is relevant and dominant in economic activities, the newly emergent caste groupings continue to play a dominant role.

As far as the economic activities are concerned the Nair and Nadar agriculturalists in the three villages are found to invoke caste affiliation for getting the support of the members of their respective castes particularly in carrying out agricultural operations.

In Kollal village all agriculturalists are Nadars. The hitherto Nair land lords have been reduced to the status of middle class peasants and agricultural workers. As the Nairs have lost their economic dominance to the Nadars who were almost exclusively dependant on them till the fourties, there emerged considerable antagonism between the Nairs and Nadars. It is mainly because of this that the relations have become strained between these two castes in this village. The Nairs who are now conscious of their economic dependance on Nadars are striving to better their condition particularly by giving better education to their children. But such an effort is mostly confined to the middle class peasants among them. Those who have become agricultural workers are greatly dissatisfied with their condition and they often create dituations of tension between the two communities by picking up quarrels with the Nadar agriculturalists and peasants during agricultural seasons. Recently, the incidence of such conflicts have become more frequent. This is probably because the Nairs in this village have emerged as an organised group.

Such aggressive postures on the part of Nairs toward Nadars particularly agriculturalists among them have been beneficial for Nadar agriculturalists. As there are two rival groups among them, the weaker group has tried to get the support of Nairs who opposed the dominant group. At the same time the dominant group headed by those agriculturalists who own and control the bulk of the land has been able to get the support of the majority of the Nadar peasants and agricultural workers in the name of caste solidarity. In short caste membership facilitates the economic activities of Nadar agriculturalists and peasants and the Nair peasants. Though the agricultural workers among both Nadars and Nairs also believe that the caste membership has been beneficial for safeguarding economic interests, in reality, they do not derive

any benefit at all. On the other hand, in the name of caste membership, they are exploited, because they do not claim better wages and very often they work for nominal wages in the name of helping their caste brethren who are the agriculturalists and peasants.

Again it is in the name of caste that the agriculturalists in the village are able to control the political activities of the rest in the name of caste affiliation. As far as the social life of the village is concerned there is little interaction between Nairs and Nadars. The social life is confined to respective castes. In marriages and other functions only those who belong to one's own caste are invited. The only exception among the Nadars are found to be with respect to three richest agriculturalists' families including that of the panchayat member. Only they invite Nairs for social functions like marriage. But even such invitations are extended only to two leading peasant families amnog Nairs who provided political leadership for the local Nairs.

In the case of Nairs, the situation is in no way different. Only the two leading peasant families invite Nadars for functions like marriage. All others in the village limit their social interaction to their respective castes. In the case of political activities the Nairs stand as a united group and during the last two Panchayat elections they have voted as a group for the present Panchayat Member who is a Nadar agriculturalist. The two leading families among them were able to derive a certain amount of economic benefits when they succeeded in giving the organized support of Nairs to the present Panchayat member.

Education is another important area where caste membership is believed to be useful. Both Nadars and Nairs believe that their respective caste membership has greatly facilitated their educational activities. But it may be pointed out that such benefits have accured only to the agriculturalists and peasants and not to agricultural workers. Even in this, the benefits went only to very few families who were able to send their children for higher education. The benefits are mostly by

way of getting admissions in the Colleges run by Nadar and Nair managements. Inspite of the fact that only very few were able to derive any benefit in the educational field, most of the Nairs and Nadars believe that the caste membership facilitate their educational activities.

As far as the Pulayas in the village are concerned, the caste membership seems to facilitate their economic activities. The caste solidarity, which is gradually emerging, has enabled them to ask for better wages and better treatment from the agriculturalists and peasants. As they are only comparatively few in number they are unable to take any decisive stand for safeguarding their economic interests. At present there is more frequent interaction among them and the earlier divisions have disappeared.

During the last Panchayat elections they made an attempt to stand united in exercising their franchise. But this attempt failed because of their numerical inferiority and the economic dependence on Nadar agriculturalists. Nevertheless they believe that caste membership facilitates their economic activities.

In the educational field, caste membership provides greater advantages to the Pulayas. The Pulaya children who are sent to school can secure stipend from the Government. They are given free meals at their schools. Probably as a result of this, majority of the Pulayas believe that caste membership facilitates their educational activities. But it may be noted that, inspite of such monetary incentives, the Pulaya children never complete the primary stage of education and are sent for agricultural work from the early age of even twelve. In other words, Pulayas are not availing the educational facilities even though there are a number of incentives for them. The reason for this is their poverty and the consequent necessity to send their children for work instead of sending them to schools.

In the Vavara village also, both Nairs and Nadars are found to believe that the caste membership facilitates their economic activities. But the real beneficiaries in both sections are the agriculturalists and, to a certain extent, the middle class

peasants. The respective caste affiliations have prevented the emergence of any class solidarity among the agricultural workers. The rivalry between the Nadars and Nairs have percolated down to all levels and as a result of this, the Nadar and Nair agricultural workers are attached to the agriculturalists belonging to their respective castes. Though the Nair agriculturalists still continue to own large tracts of land, the emergence of Nadar agriculturalists and peasants, by taking over land belonging to a large section of Nairs, have made the Nairs quite hostile and suspicious of Nadars as a whole. As in Kollal village, in Vavara village also, there are frequent incidence of conflicts between the two communities. The hostility towards Nadars are mostly confined to the peasants and agricultural workers among the Nairs. Such conflicts occur mostly during agricultural seasons and at the time of temple festivals. There is also frequent land disputes between Nadar agriculturalists and Nair peasants. Though such disputes are purely personal and over certain specific plots of land, yet other members of the caste who are not parties to such disputes also actively take part in the name of caste. Recently there were two incidents in which the land disputes between two Nair and Nadar agriculturalists have resulted into overt physical violence and assaults between the two communities as a whole. Strangely enough, apart from the two agriculturalists, most of the other participants in these two instances of conflicts were the agricultural workers who were not to benefit from such disputes.

On the whole, it can be said that the caste membership and caste consciousness function for a safeguarding the economic interests of agriculturalists and peasants. At the same time they facilitate the exploitation of agricultural workers. This is because, even though the wage in the village is very small and inadequate, the agriculturalists always try to secure the services of the agricultural workers of their respective caste for still smaller wage. They often succeed because the appeal is always in the name of caste. Also the caste cleavages and caste consciousness among the agricultural workers have effectively prevented the emergence of class solidarity among them.

The social life in the village is also on the basis of caste affiliations. In social functions like marriage, caste members alone take part. But such caste divisions are mostly confined to the middle class peasants and agricultural workers. As far as the agriculturists among both Nadars and Nairs are concerned they invite each other for social functions like marriage, resulting into greater interactions among them. Nevertheless bulk of social interactions are confined to the respective castes and the inter-group relations are confined to only a few families of agriculturists in both castes.

The caste membership greatly facilitates the political activities in the village. Compared to other villages, the Nairs in this village are better organized and are led by the agriculturists among them. Similarly it is the agriculturists among Nadars who provided the necessary leadership for that caste in the village. During the last Panchayat elections there were two contestants and both of them were agriculturists. But one of them was a Nadar and the other was a Nair. The caste feelings have reached the zenith during this election. The Nairs, as a whole, voted for the Nair candidates and the Nadars, on their turn, stood solidly behind the Nadar contestant. The support of Pulayas was more or less evenly divided between the two contestants and as the Nadars are numerically superior, Nadar contestant has won the election. Thus it can be seen that caste division between Nairs and Nadars extends to the political life. Though most of the Nadars and Nairs believe that their caste affiliations enable them to safeguard their political interests, it is the agriculturists among them who derive benefits. There is practically no benefit for the agricultural workers in the two castes.

Both Nadars and Nairs believe that the caste membership enables them to safeguard their educational interests. But as in the case of economic and political activities, only agriculturists and peasants derive any benefit. Quite a few of them are able to secure facilities for higher education for their children by virtue of their caste affiliations. But the agricultural workers belonging to the two castes could not secure

any such benefit. Therefore it can be said that though caste membership is believed to facilitate educational activities such facilitations tend to confine mostly to upper class agriculturists and to a lesser extent to the middle class peasantry.

As far as the Pulayas in the village are concerned, with the emergence of solidarity among them, caste solidarity is found to be useful for safeguarding their economic interests. As all of them are agricultural workers and as the emergent caste solidarity binds them together they are now in a position to bargain for better wages from the agriculturists and peasants who employ them. As most of them are attached to agriculturists they have succeeded in securing better wages and better treatment by standing united. But this is a recent development and at present the wages given to the Pulayas in this village are much higher than the wages given to the agricultural workers in the Kollal village. The success which the Pulayas achieved in securing better wages with the emergence of only a semblance of unity among them have initiated more vigorous efforts for bringing them still more close. They are on the verge of emerging as a well organized group.

In the social life also there is greater interaction among them. All divisions among them have disappeared and there is greater social co-operation. It is because of this that they believe in the efficacy of caste membership in facilitating social activities.

As far as the political activities of the Pulayas are concerned they are yet to stand as a united group. Though some attempts toward this direction have been made during the last Panchayat elections, the acute rivalry between Nadars and Nairs resulted in splitting the Pulaya votes between the two contestants. The economic dominance of the Nair and Nadar agriculturists enabled them to command considerable influence among the Pulaya agricultural workers and it is this that enabled them to split the Pulayas between the two contestants. But the present trend towards greater organization and unity among Pulayas show that such split may not occur in future.

Though there are a number of monetary incentives like stipends, mid-day meals etc., for encouraging Pulayas to acquire higher education, there was no significant improvement in their educational status. They do not send their children beyond primary stage, even though stipends and scholarships are available. Even when the children are in primary stage, parents encourage them to take up agricultural work. Though all of them believe that their caste membership facilitate educational activities there are none among them who have secured any real benefit.

Though traditional caste stratification has been replaced by caste groupings caste affiliations are still considered to be an important factor in the socio-economic, political and educational life of Viakkalloor village.

As far as the Nairs are concerned, the caste affiliation is considered to be a significant factor in promoting their economic activities. Though the economic benefits that accrue from caste affiliation and caste solidarity go mostly to the Nair agriculturists and such benefits are only nominal in the case of Nair peasants, the peasantry among them also feel that caste affiliation facilitates their economic activities. As far as the agriculturists are concerned, with the growing tension between Nadars and Nairs, they find it difficult to carry on agricultural operations, when Nadars as a whole are hostile to them. When situations of tension arise during agricultural seasons between Nair agriculturists and Nadar workers, the Nair peasants invariably rally around the Nair agriculturists. Recently there were three such instances of tension between the two communities. Though the parties who are really involved were two agriculturists and their Nadar workers, on all the three occasions the Nair peasantry came forward to help the agriculturists and only the timely intervention by the police saved the situation from developing into physical violence.

It may be noted that the agriculturists could secure support from the peasantry merely on the basis of caste affiliations. In fact, none of the peasants who were involved in these conflicts derived any economic benefit. Yet majority of them believe

that caste affiliation enables them to safeguard their economic interests though it is only the agriculturists, who have benefitted from such caste affiliations.

The social life of Nairs in the village is almost exclusively confined to their own caste. In various social functions like marriage only Nairs alone are invited. At present when a marriage is settled the parties involved inform the Karayogam officially and once this is done all Nair families in the village help the parties concerned in conducting the marriage. In the case of agriculturists, all Nair in the village are invited for their marriages. But in the case of peasants, only a few decided upon by the Karayogam need be invited. The number of persons thus invited varies depending on the economic status of the parties concerned.

Close co-operation exists among Nairs in organizing the temple festivals of the village. They share the expenditure and at present the festivals are organised by the Karayogam.

Another important factor that facilitates a high frequency of social interaction among the Nairs is the periodical meetings of the Karayogam itself Once in every month all adult Nairs in the village meet and discuss social problems which the community as a whole confronts in the village. During such gatherings individual disputes between members are also settled. After the organization of Karayogam in 1970, even the land disputes between Nairs were never permitted to reach litigation stage. Also one litigation that existed before 1970 between two Nair agriculturists was settled outside the Court after the organization of Karayogam.

As far as the political activities are concerned the Nairs stand as a united group. During the last Panchayat election it was the Karayogam which met and decided as to the political stand which they have to take. As the Nairs are united and as they form quite a sizeable section of the population in the village they continue to have decisive influence in the political life of the village even after Independence. Also their economic dominance enabled them to control the political behaviour

of Pulayas and a section of Nadars. It was a result of this that the Nair candidate could always win the Panchayat elections in the village. Here again it is to be noted that the caste solidarity in political life has benefitted only the Nair agriculturists. It was always an agriculturist who used to get elected and his primary concern, all along, has been to safeguard the economic interests of the Nair agriculturists. Therefore, it may be said that the caste solidarity in political activities tend to benefit only the upper class in the caste.

As far as the educational activities are concerned, the Nairs in the village believe that their caste affiliations have enabled them to derive educational benefits. The agriculturists among them could send their children for collegiate education and most of them could secure seats in colleges under the management of the Nair Service Society. In securing admissions, it is the caste affiliations and their economic affluence that helped them. As far as the Nair peasants are concerned, only two families among them could send their children to College. In both cases, the children joined the Government College and as such their caste affiliations did not play any crucial role. This, in a way, shows that the educational benefits that are derived through caste affiliations go mainly in favour of the upper class. Even though the peasantry among them could not derive many benefits, they also are found to believe that caste affiliations have enabled them to improve their educational status.

Even before the pre-Independent days Nadars in the Village were well-organized and the Caste Panchayat enabled them to stand united. After political Independence, the emergence of Nadars as a powerful group in South Travancore Region has affected the life of Nadars in this village also. When a few among them (Nine families) have emerged as middle class peasants and ceased to be economically dependant on Nairs, they started trying to improve their economic status by competing with Nair agriculturists and peasants This situation arose mainly when the land legislations enabled those families to take over some of the land which they were cultivating as tenants of Nairs. When they got ownership over such lands,

they simultaneously staked claim on some of the lands which belonged to the Nair agriculturists. They claimed that they were cultivating these lands as tenants and as such they should get the ownership over them also. This situation led to a number of disputes between Nadar peasants and Nair agriculturists. With the help of other Nadars, they forcibly occupied the land under dispute. But the Nair agriculturist forcibly evicted them. Though these disputes were settled by the middle of the fifties itself, the strained relations between these two communities continued and have reached a climax at present. Very often land disputes arise between Nadar peasants and Nair agriculturists and peasants. In all land disputes involving Nadar peasants, the agricultural workers among Nadars also take part. It is due to this that the Nair agriculturists have started employing only Pulayas for agricultural work. At present both peasants and agriculturists among Nairs do not employ Nadars for agricultural operations. As a result of this, the local agricultural workers among Nadars find it difficult to get employment in the village and hence they are forced to seek employment in neighbouring villages. When they go outside the village seeking employment they often do not get any and as such the Nadar workers are reduced to adject poverty. The only economic beneficiary from the caste solidarity and caste affiliation among them are the peasants. On the other hand, the caste solidarity has adversely affected the economic interests of the agricultural workers who constitute the large majority among them. Also this caste unity has prevented the Nadar agricultural workers from uniting with the Pulaya labourers. In spite of this, the Nadars as a whole believe that caste membership enables them to safeguard their economic interests.

The social life of Nadars is almost exclusively confined to their own caste. Their caste Panchayat brings them together thereby fostering a high frequency of social interaction among them. All disputes among them are settled by the Panchayat and with the emergence of conflict between them and Nairs, intra-caste disputes have become less frequent.

In organizing marriage functions close co-operation is found among the Nadars. It is through caste Panchayat that marriage functions are organized. The caste solidarity may become more manifest when a crisis like death occurs. When some one dies in a family, both peasants and agricultural workers among them join together to help the bereaved family. It is the caste Panchayat that organizes the temple festivals. The initiative for this comes from the peasants among them and the agricultural workers make as much contribution as they can for making the festivals a success.

The unity among the Nadars can be seen in their political life also. Till the last Panchayat elections they never used to play only a passive role. But during the last Panchayat elections one of the peasants among the Nadars stood as a candidate to oppose the Nair contestant. But he failed to get any support from the Pulayas though he could secure majority of Nadar votes. This election served to unite the Nadars in the political field though they could not win the elections. Though both peasants and agricultural workers among Nadars believe that caste solidarity among them serve to safeguard their political interests, it has benefitted only a few peasants among them. As far as the workers are concerned caste solidarity has only alienated them from the Pulaya agricultural workers.

In the educational field, Nadars are yet to make any significant stride. Only the middle class peasant families could succeed in providing High School education for their children. As far as the agricultural workers among them are concerned, they do not give education for their children beyond the primary stage. As far as the Collegiate education is concerned, only one Nadar peasant family could send the children for collegiate education. In this case the family could secure seats in the College managed by the L.M.S. Mission. It was their caste affiliation that has enabled them to secure seats in the College. Though educational benefits that have been derived by Nadars through their caste affiliations are negligible, they believe that such affiliations could foster their interests in the field of education.

Though the Pulayas in Viakkalloor village constitute the most dominant numerical section of the population, all of them continue to be agricultural workers. They were the 'Adians' of the Nair landlords in the early days and as the Nair monopoly over the land continued even after political Independence, there was no significant change in the traditional allegiance which the Pulayas had towards the Nairs. Till the fourties, there were two sections among Pulayas owing allegiance to two Nair joint families. After the partition of these families, when the traditional Nair landlords became agriculturists, Pulayas continued to owe allegiance to them None of the Pulayas own any land and all of them live in Cheris which belong to Nair agriculturists. As far as the employment prospects of Pulayas are concerned, they are totally dependant on Nair agriculturists and peasants. They never give any opportunity for any strained relations to develop between them and Nairs. When the Nair agriculturists refused to employ Nadar labour, the importance of Pulayas in carrying out agricultural operations in the village has considerably gone up. Though the Nair agriculturists and peasants have become more dependant on Pulayas in cultivating their land, so far, the Pulayas have not made any attempt to take advantage of the situation by asking for better wages and better working conditions. They consider the Nadar workers as their rivals and, as such, they have been willing to work for lesser wages if it could prevent the Nadar workers from being employed by the Nair agriculturists. The rivalry between Nadar and Pulaya workers have, in a way, benefitted the Nair agriculturists and peasants because, by excluding the Nadar labourers they could secure the services of Pulaya workers at low wages. At the same time it may be noted that a certain amount of unity is gradually emerging among the Pulayas as a result of the rivalry between them and the Nadar workers. During the last one year the adult Pulayas of the village met five times to discuss various tactics that were to be employed for preventing the Nadar workers from being employed in any of the land belonging to the Nair agriculturists and peasants. Though the primary purpose for these gatherings was to discuss this problem, of late, there has been a tendency to discuss other social and economic problems as well. But they have never

even discussed anything that will enable them to demand better wages from the Nair employers.

It is probably because of this emergent unity that the Pulayas could prevent the rival Nadar workers from being employed in the village. It is probably on account of this that they believe in the efficacy of caste affiliations in fostering their economic interests. It can be stated that the emergent caste solidarity among Pulayas is simultaneously fostering solidarity among the agricultural workers as it is Pulayas who constitute the majority of workers. As there are no agriculturists or middle class peasants among them, the caste solidarity has fostered the interests of only the agricultural workers.

Social life of Pulayas is confined to their own caste. Before the abolition of untouchability and other social distance practices they did not have even physical access to the village and as such they were compelled to lead an isolated social life confined to their own caste. Even after political Independence no significant change has taken place in the pattern of social activities among them. They live in Cheris which are located outside the village proper and as soon as the day's work is over in the field they go back to the Cheris and not to the village. Only for buying their necessities they visit the village and otherwise all their activities are confined to their community settlements. There is close co-operation among them in the social activities of the Cheris.

As far as the political activities of Pulayas are concerned, it is the Nair agriculturists and peasants who influence and direct them. Though the Pulayas form the most numerically dominant section of the population and as such by standing united they could always win any election in the village, so far, they have never made any attempt in this direction. During all Panchayat elections, they have been faithfully toeing the lead given by the Nairs. They merely exercise their franchise as per the direction of the Nair agriculturists. During the last Panchayat elections, when the contest was between a Nair and Nadar, they gave their votes to the Nair candidate. It is as a result of this that the Nair candidate could easily win the elec-

tions defeating the Nadar contestant. So far, such a united stand by Pulayas in political activities has benefitted only the Nairs. But the new unity that is emerging among Pulayas may ultimately enable them to free themselves from the Nair influence. Most of them believe that their caste membership facilitates their political activities.

As far as the educational field is concerned, Pulayas are yet to make any significant progress. Though there are a number of monetary incentives like stipends and scholarships for Pulaya children, they have not made use of these educational opportunities. The education of their children stop short of primary stage and even before the children become adolescents, they are inducted into various work roles. There are none among the local Pulayas who had secured high school education. In spite of this lack of any educational achievement the Pulayas are found to believe that their caste membership facilitates their eduational activities.

As already pointed out, though the hierarchical caste stratification has been replaced by horizontal caste groupings, caste affiliations continue to play a dominant role in the socio-economic and political life of the village. Caste continues to provide the only basis for kinship relations like marriage. There are none in the three villages who dare to transgress the caste boundry in contracting marriages. There are none in the three villages who dare to transgress the caste boundry in contracting marriages. Also caste preference is shown by majority of Nairs, Nadars and Pulayas in contracting personal relationship. It is interesting to note that those who do not show caste preferences in personal friendship belongs to the upper class agriculturists and middle class peasants even though it is they who provide caste leadership in all the three villages. Similarly neighbourhood preferences are, mostly, for those who belong to one's own caste.

Caste Stereotypes

The competitive and conflicting relations between Nairs and Nadars in the three villages have led to the emergence of caste stereotypes. It is found that Nairs attribute all unfavourable

TABLE 9
Stereotypes of Nairs[8]

Castes	*Crooked*	*Unscrupulous*	*Straight Forward*	*Stingy*	*Large hearted*	*Religious minded*	*Communal*	*Total*
Nairs	9 (12.16%)	4 (5.40%)	39 (52.71%)	7 (9.46%)	7 (9.46%)	7 (9.46%)	1 (1.35%)	74 (100%)
Nadars	38 (33.62%)	13 (11.50%)	40 (35.40%)	6 (5.31%)	9 (7.96%)	5 (4.43%)	2 (1.78%)	113 (100%)
Pulayas	3 (5%)	5 (8.33%)	40 (66.66%)	3 (5%)	3 (5%)	4 (6.67%)	2 (3.34%)	60 (100%)
Total	50 (20.25%)	22 (8.91%)	119 (48.17%)	16 (6.47%)	19 (7.69%)	16 (6.47%)	5 (2.02%)	247 (100%)

$X^2 = 67.7094$ $X^2_{.99(12)} = 26.22$

Significant at 1% level.

TABLE 10

Stereotypes of Nadars[9]

Castes	Crooked	Unscrupulous	Straight forward	Stingy	Large hearted	Religious minded	Communal	Total
Nairs	27 (36.50%)	4 (5.40%)	14 (18.91%)	21 (28.38%)	6 (8.11%)	1 (1.35%)	1 (1.35%)	74 (100%)
Nadars	17 (15.04%)	7 (6.19%)	47 (41.59%)	21 (18.59%)	5 (7.08%)	8 (7.08%)	5 (4.43%)	113 (100%)
Pulayas	20 (33.32%)	7 (11.66%)	16 (26.67%)	12 (20%)	1 (1.67%)	2 (3.34%)	2 (3.34%)	60 (100%)
Total	64 (25.92%)	18 (7.29%)	77 (31.19%)	54 (21.87%)	15 (6.08%)	11 (4.46%)	8 (3.17%)	247 (100%)

$X^2 = 99 \cdot 5129$ $X^2_{.99(12)} = 26.22$

Significant at 1% level.

TABLE 11

Stereotypes of Pulayas[10]

Castes	*Crooked*	*Unscrupulous*	*Straight forward*	*Stingy*	*Large hearted*	*Religious minded*	*Communal*	*Total*
Nairs	2	6	27	4	8	14	13	74
	(2.70%)	(8.11%)	(36.50%)	(5.40%)	(10.80%)	(18.92%)	(17.57%)	(100%)
Nadars	3	9	47	3	17	26	8	113
	(2.66%)	(7.97%)	(41.59%)	(2.65%)	(15.04%)	(23.01%)	(7.08%)	(100%)
Pulayas	1	5	32	1	5	7	9	60
	(1.67%)	(8.33%)	(53.34%)	(1.67%)	(8.33%)	(11.65%)	(15%)	(100%)
Total	6	20	106	8	30	47	30	247
	(2.45%)	(8.11%)	(42.92%)	(3.18%)	(12.15%)	(19.04%)	(12.15%)	(100%)

$X^2 = 13.9702$ $X^2_{.99(12)} = 26.22$

Not significant at 1% level.

and undesirable characteristics on Nadars. Similarly Nadars also believe that all undesirable and unfavourable characteristics are found in Nairs. As far as the members of one's own community are concerned, all favourable and desirable characteristics are attributed to them. As the Pulayas in all the three villages are dependant on either Nairs or Nadars, in all fields, the stereotypes regarding them are found to be favourable ones. But there are a few undesirable and unfavourable characteristics that are attributed to both Nadars and Nairs by the Pulayas. This is probably because they are gradually realizing that they are exploited by the upper class Nairs and Nadars.

Though the traditional caste stratification as such as no more prevalent, the villagers prefer to retain the caste and sectarian cleavages among them. They are found to believe that the caste system is necessary for safeguarding the traditional values and also for safeguarding the economic and political interests of each caste. But the caste system which they want to retain is the caste associations rather than hierarchical caste system. It is found that the existence of caste association in this village prevents the emergence of class consciousness among the weaker sections of the three major castes. In a way, the prevalent caste associations are found to promote only the economic, political and educational interests of upper caste sections among Nairs and Nadars. Though majority among each caste for found to be aware of the fact that the caste associations do not help them in any way in promoting their economic interests, yet, the economic prosperity among a small section of Nairs and Nadars make them believe that caste associations may promote the economic interests of the lower classes in such castes also. It is probably this belief among the majority of the lower class Nairs (21), Nadars (70) and Pulayas (40) that make them unfavourable to a casteless society.

NOTES

1. Yogendra Singh, "Caste and Class : Some aspects of Continuity and Change", Sociological Bulletin, Journal of the Indian Sociological Society, Vol. XVII, September 1968, No. 2, p. 169.

2. Radhakamal Mukerjee, "Caste Distance and Tension in the village", from "Inter Caste Tensions : A Survey under the auspicious of UNESCO", University of Lucknow, 1951, p. 6.
3. *Ibid* , p. 19.
4. *Ibid* , Q. III-7 (iv).
5. *Ibid*., Q. III-7 (v).
6. *Ibid* , Q. III-(a).
7. *Ibid*., Q. III-19 (i).
8. *Ibid*., Q. III-19 (i).
9. *Ibid*., Q. III (19) (ii).
10. *Ibid*., Q. III-11 (iii).

Chapter Five

CASTE STRATIFICATION AND CHANGING VALUE SYSTEM

Every society has a value system distinctive to its social and economic needs. In the traditional Indian society, value system was for ensuring the smooth functioning of the caste system. The lower castes were to be kept in subordination to the upper castes and social distance practices such as untouchability were the effective means for perpetuating the subordination. Value system in the traditional society made the lower castes to "live outside the village in unspeakable filth, eking out their existence by menial and polluting labour... In dry areas they find it difficult to find water for bathing and even for drinking... Their touch, their very presence is thought to contaminate others.... The 1931 census spoke of their being debarred from the use of tax supported roads, from temples, burning grounds and other religious institutions, and from private tea shops, hotels and theatres ...".[1]

Religion used to play an important role in the value system. Religious faiths and beliefs held the value system in tact. Religious faiths and beliefs, which held the value system in tact, was man's self-consciousness and self-awareness in the traditional society.[2] But the traditional value system was essentially a product of the differential distribution pattern of scarce values and the attendant caste stratification.

Economy and Traditional Value System

In all the three villages, the traditional hierarchical caste stratification used to conform to the distribution pattern of the scarce values of land. The Nairs who constituted the highest caste, owned and controlled almost the entire land wealth. Both Nadars and Pulayas did not have any share in the scarce value of land. But the caste status of Nadars was higher than that of Pulayas. Though majority of Nadars were agricultural labour like Pulayas, there was a section among them who assisted the Nair landlords in cultivating the land in supervisory capacities. Subsequently, when the Nair joint families were partitioned, quite a few among Nadars became tenants. Also there were a few among them who were middle class traders. This presence of a comparatively affluent section among them provided a higher status for the caste as a whole. As the Pulayas were exclusively agriculture wage labour, they were placed at the bottom of the caste hierarchy.

But the near total Nair monopoly over land and almost total exclusion of Nadars and Pulayas from land ownership gave a dichotomous character to the traditional caste system. The caste Hindus were constituted only by Nairs. Both Nadars and Pulayas were untouchables. This dichotomous division of caste seems to be a consequence of the different and distribution pattern of the scarce value of land. As the cultivation was predominantly paddy, there was a necessity for sustained supply of cheap labour for the paddy cultivation. It was probably this economic necessity that accounted for the emergence of Pulaya caste who used to be kept as semi-slaves attached to Nair lords. Nairs, who constituted a small minority of the total population in the villages could not, by themselves cultivate a major portion of their land wealth. It is in order to overcome this difficulty that a few among the Nadars were elevated to the middle class status by giving them supervisory functions in agricultural activities. Also, they were assigned a higher status compared to Pulaya labour. It is, probably, under these circumstances that the intermediary caste of Nadars has emerged in between the Pulaya agricultural labour and Nair landlords.

Value System

The traditional value system was essentially for perpetuating these superstructural arrangements for reinforcing the differential distribution pattern of the scarce value of land. Untouchability and pollution used to be practised in a severe form by the Nairs so as to keep the Nadars and the Pulayas at their respective subordinate positions in the social, political and cultural fields as in the case of economic field. The Nadars were shown more laxity as to the various social distance practices. As some of them who had the supervisory and trading functions were to associate closely with the Nair landlords, they used to be permitted to move about on public roads and thoroughfares. They were to keep only a few feet of distance from Nairs and were only to give way for Nairs as and when they meet on the roads. But in the case of Pulayas, the social distance practices were very severe. They were never permitted to use the public thoroughfares. Also they had to keep a shouting distance from Nairs and also had to keep a few feet of physical distance from Nadars. Interdining was confined only to one's own caste. The traditional beliefs and attitudes were also for fostering this super-ordinate-subordinate caste relations. The belief in rebirth and fate helped the members of various castes to reconcile themselves with their respective economic and social conditions.

But, when the differential distribution pattern of the scarce values of land ceased to synchronize with the traditional caste stratification, many of the traditional values, beliefs and attitudes which reinforced the caste system have undergone considerable change. In Vavara and Kollal villages, when the Nadars became land proprietors like Nairs, the traditional social distance practices for keeping the Nadars in subordinate socio-economic positions ceased to be of any relevance. In Kollal village, the economic status of Nadars has surpassed the upper caste Nairs relegating the latter to subordinate positions. Nairs came to be economically dependant on Nadars In the Vavara village also the Nadars are found to possess more or less the same economic status as the Nairs. Under the circumstances, the traditional social distance practices have become almost an

anarchism. In the case of Viakkalloor village, though their is no corresponding economic prosperity for Nadars, the change in their economic status in the larger society had their impact on various social distance practices and concerned beliefs and values.

As a consequence to this, social interaction between the castes has become more frequent. When, in early times, those who did not belong to one's own caste used to be denied access to one's own home, by contemporary times, caste has ceased to be a basis for inviting the guests to one's own home for various functions.

TABLE 12
Preference in Inviting Members of Other Castes to One's Home[3]

Castes	*Those who invite members of other Castes*	*Those who do not invite members of other castes*	*Total*
Nairs	32 (43.24%)	42 (56.76%)	74 (100%)
Nadars	84 (74.34%)	29 (25 66%)	113 (100%)
Pulayas	43 (71.67%)	17 (28.33%)	60 (100%)
Total	159 (64.37%)	88 (35.63%)	247 (100%)

$X^2 = 20.1132 \quad X^2_{.99(2)} = 9.21$

Significant at 1% level.

As far as the social interaction between the castes are concerned, Nairs are found to be more reluctant to enter into interaction with Nadars and Pulayas. But such reluctance is found to be less among Nadars and Pulayas.

Interdining used to be confined to respective castes. But, with the gradual decline of social distance practices, and when members of other castes began to be invited to various functions in households, the restrictions on interdining gradually wained. It was found that, among the Nairs and Nadars who are relatively at par in economic status, there is little objection in

interdining between these two castes. But both Nairs and Nadars are found to be reluctant to have interdining with Pulayas (38.33 per cent and 26.67 per cent . On the other hand, Pulayas who are yet to register any appreciable improvement in their economic status are not found to have any objection in inter-dining with any caste. This, in a way, shows their anxiety to improve their economic and social status.

Compared to Nadars and Pulayas, sectarian feelings seem to be more among Nadars. Majority of Nairs are found to be averse to interdine with Nadars and Pulayas (64.86 per cent and 67.57 per cent). Though there has been a decline in their dominance in social, economic and political spheres, they are found to retain some of the traditional values and beliefs which were for reinforcing their socio-economic and political dominance. But such beliefs and values have no relevance in contemporary society, particularly in view of the economic decline of Nairs in Vavara and Kollal villages where the dominance has gone to Nadars. But former rigidity regarding inter-caste relations is not any more found

The change in the traditional beliefs and attitudes regarding social distance practices is more or less a recent development

TABLE 13

Participation of Other Castes in Family Functions During the Time of Parents[4]

Castes	*Members of other castes invited*	*Members of other castes not invited*	*Total*
Nairs	16 (21.62%)	58 (78.38%)	74 (100%)
Nadars	29 (25.66%)	84 (74.34%)	113 (100%)
Pulayas	15 (25%)	45 (75%)	60 (100%)
Total	60 (24.30%)	187 (75.70%)	247 (100%)

$X^2 = 0.4128$ $X^2_{.99(2)} = 9.21$ Not significant at 1% level.

after political Independence. The members belonging to other castes were never used to be invited for family functions. This can be seen from the fact that, a generation back, during the time of respondent's grant parents and great grand parents, members from other castes never used to participate in their family functions.

TABLE 14
Participation of Other Castes in Family Functions During the Time of Grand Parents[5]

Castes	*Members of other castes invited*	*Members of other castes not invited*	*Total*
Nairs	6 (8.11%)	68 (91.89%)	74 (100%)
Nadars	14 (12.40%)	99 (87.60%)	113 (100%)
Pulayas	9 (15%)	51 (85%)	60 (100%)
Total	29 (11.74%)	218 (88.26%)	247 (100%)

$X^2 = 1\ 7901$ $\quad X^2_{.99(2)} = 9.21$ $\quad$ Not significant at 1% level.

TABLE 15
Participation of Other Castes in Family Functions During the Time of Great Grand Parents[6]

Castes	*Members of other castes invited*	*Members of other castes not invited*	*Total*
Nairs	—	74 (100%)	74 (100%)
Nadars	4 (3.54%)	109 (96.46%)	113 (100%)
Pulayas	7 (11.66%)	53 (88.34%)	60 (100%)
Total	11 (4.46%)	236 (95.54%)	247 (100%)

$X^2 = 7.5729$ $\quad X^2_{.99\ (2)} = 9.21$ $\quad$ Not significant at 1% level.

$X^2 = 7.5729$ $\quad X^2_{.95\ (2)} = 5.99$ $\quad$ Significant at 5% level.

Though social distance practices and related beliefs and attitudes are no more found to be dominant in the three villages, compared to Pulayas and Nadars, Nairs are found to be more hesitant to give access for non-Nairs to their household premises like kitchen. In this regard, they are relatively more tolerant towards Nadars than Pulayas. This may be due to the rising economic status of Nadars. On the other hand, Nadars are found to have little objection for giving access to Nairs in their households. But they do not like to give such freedom to Pulayas. The Pulayas are found to have no objection in giving, either Nairs or Nadars, access to their households.

Both Nairs and Nadars are found to be in favour of having separate places of worship for their respective castes. The Pulayas who, till recently, used to be denied access to places of worship are found to be for common places of worship for all castes.

TABLE 16

Preference for Commonplace for Worship[7]

Castes	*Prefer common place of worship*	*Do not prefer common place of worship*	*Total*
Nairs	36 (48.64%)	38 (51.36%)	74 (100%)
Nadars	38 (33.63%)	75 (66.37%)	113 (100%)
Pulayas	41 (68.33%)	19 (31.67%)	60 (100%)
Total	115 (46.56%)	132 (53.44%)	247 (100%)

$X^2 = 11.7809$ $X^2_{.99(2)} = 9.21$ Significant at 1% level.

Religious Faith and Changing Value System

Faith in god or supernatural power is found to be widely prevalent among the villagers.[8] It was such beliefs that sustained the caste and sectarian stratification in the traditional society. But these beliefs are no more as strong as in the old

days. Till recently, some kind of supernatural blessings used to be invoked at the time of sowing, harvesting etc. Those rituals were usually in the form of poojas or services at temples or churches and some kind of donation either in cash or kind for worshipping centres. But at present such practices are only rarely found among Nairs and Nadars while they still persist among the Pulayas. The declining faith in supernatural power among Nairs and Nadars reflect the changing economic status of these two sections. These practices persist only among the Pulayas (83.34 per cent). This is probably because they are the only sections in the three villages who continue to stagnate as far as their socio-economic conditions are concerned. Therefore it can be said that when the distribution pattern of scarce values undergoes change, it tends to bring about corresponding changes in the social and religious backgrounds.

In the traditional society an important belief, which helped in inhibiting any intra-structural challenge to the gross differential distribution of scarce values, was the faith in supernatural powers and the beliefs in rebirth and fate. The beliefs in rebirth and fate facilitated the exploitation of the wage labour consisting of Nadars and Pulayas by the upper caste Nairs. Both Nadars (74.34 per cent) and Pulayas (66.67 per cent) used to believe that it was God who created the difference in the social and economic status of people, and it was their fate that they should be in perpetual subordination and subjection. They also believed that, if they reconciled to their fate without any revolt or protest, God would provide them with a higher caste status during subsequent births. These beliefs and values safeguarded the economic interests of the upper caste Nairs against any possible threats from the low caste Nadars and Pulayas.

But the political Independence, adult franchise and the recognition of equality before the law shattered the sacred basis for the monopolistic control of land by Nair landlords. Though Nairs could retain the ownership over land during pre-Independent days, they ceased to exercise any control over the land subsequent to political Independence. The various land reform legislations vested the possession and control of land

on Nadar tenants. Thus the economic foundation for the hierarchical caste system in the three villages disappeared and the natural consequence was the declining influence of traditional beliefs and values which supported the Nair monopoly over land.

Both Nairs and Nadars in the three villages recognised the importance of one's own effort as against fate in shaping their socio-economic life. This growing recognition of one's own capacity to change the social and economic conditions as against leaving them in the hands of supernatural power is symptomatic of the economic changes that are taking place in the villages.

The traditional belief was that the upper caste Nairs alone could own land and wield social and political power. But, when the Nadars could gradually secure control and ownership over the land, it was realised that they also could improve their economic status and such change would be merely a consequence of one's own effort and not something willed by any supernatural power. Compared to Nairs, it is the Nadars who rely more on their own effort to improve their socio-economic status. As far as the Pulayas are concerned, there has been very little change in their socio-economic status. The only change, that has taken place, was the shift in their allegiance from Nairs to Nadars in Kollal and Vavara villages. Otherwise they continued to be economically and socially dependant on the concerned upper class sections in each of the three villages. In Kollal village the Pulayas are attached to Nadar agriculturists. In the Vavara village their allegiance is more or less evenly divided between Nairs and Nadars. In Viakkalloor village they continue to be subservient to Nairs. It has become the economic necessity for the upper class sections among both Nadars and Nairs that the Pulayas should be kept in socio-economic subservience so as to ensure a sustained supply of cheap labour for agricultural operations. Consequently, there is little opportunity for Pulayas in the three villages to go in for higher education and employment other than agricultural operations. This persistence of traditional conditions in the socio-economic life of Pulayas accounts for

the persisting faith among them in the fate alone as the sole factor that determines the socio-economic conditions of people. They reconcile to their hand to mouth existence and the exploitation of their labour by upper caste Nadars and Nairs by firmly believing that it was due to their fate. As they have little opportunity to improve their socio-economic life, they do not believe that they would be able to improve their condition through their own effort. It is this attitude on the part of Pulayas that make them pessimistic towards the future. On the other hand the growing affluence of a sizeable section among them makes the Nadars more optimistic regarding their future. But at the same time, it is the declining socio-economic status of Nairs that is reflected in their pessimistic attitudes about future.

As far as the religious ceremonies are concerned, they are performed only occasionally by Nairs and Nadars. But compared to Nairs, religious faith seems to be more strong among Nadars. But the Pulayas are found to be very religious and hence are quite regular in observing ceremonies. But the religious faith is found to be gradually on the decline in the three villages. Till two decades ago, participation in worship in religious centres used to be always mandatory among the villagers. But this regular participation has become only occasional at present. Though the religious faith is gradually on the decline among all the villagers except Pulayas, a marked decline can be seen among the younger generation. It is particularly more among Nairs and Pulayas.

TABLE 17

Celebration of Religious Ceremonies[9]

Castes	*Regularly*	*Occasionally*	*Never*	*Total*
Nairs	14 (18.92%)	58 (78.38%)	2 (2.70%)	74 (100%)
Nadars	32 (28.32%)	77 (68.15%)	4 (3.54%)	113 (100%)
Pulayas	44 (73.33%)	13 (21.67%)	3 (5%)	60 (100%)
Total	90 (36.43%)	148 (59.93%)	9 (3.64%)	247 (100%)

$X^2 = 30.6277$ $X^2_{.99}(4) = 13.28$

Significant at 1% level.

NOTES

1. Manson Olcott, "The Caste System of India", American Sociological Review, December 1944 : Vol. 9, No. 6, The Official Journal of the American Sociological Society, p. 649.
2. M.N. Srinivas, "Religion and Society among the Coorgs in South India", Oxford University Press, 1952
3. Appendix-I. Q. IX-1.
4. *Ibid.*, Q. IX-4 (*i*).
5. *Ibid* , Q. IX-4 (*ii*).
6. *Ibid* , Q. IX-4 (*iii*).
7. *Ibid* , Q. IX-6.
8. *Ibid.*, Q. IX-8.
9. *Ibid.*, Q. VIII-4.

Chapter Six

CLASS STRATIFICATION

Though class stratification in some form or other is found in all societies, the nature of such stratification differs depending on the economy of the country, the type of labour its people perform, the communities in which they live and the social relations into which they enter. Thus "Every social class is a special social organism, living, acting and suffering as such and in need of being understood as such"[1] or in other words "a class is aware of its identity as a whole, sublimates itself as such, has its own peculiar life and characteristic spirit."[2]

People belonging to a particular group, consciously or unconsciously feel the unity of oneness and they behave as a group. So also the group will be ranked in the society in socially superior and inferior positions according to its characteristics

Social interactions between the members of a group will be greater and the inter-class relation will be minimal. People will be reluctant to become close with people who are inferior to them, at the same time they try to imitate the upper class people. It is because of this that class is often considered as a socio-psychological factor.[3]

Sorokin sums up the characteristics of classes as "(1) legally open, but actually semi-closed ; (2) normal ; (3) solitary ;

(4) antagonistic to certain other groups (social classes) of the same general nature ; (5) partially organized but mainly quasi-organised ; (6) partly aware of its own unity and existence and partly not ... ; (8) multibounded group bound together by two unibond ties—occupational and economic (both taken in their broad sense) and by one bond of social stratification in the sense of the totality of its essential rights and duties as contrasted with the essentially different rights and duties of other groups (Social classes) of the general nature".[4]

In the traditional Indian Society class stratification used to synchronize with caste stratification. The upper classes of society was the upper castes and the low caste Shudras and outcastes constituted the lower classes. The pattern was no different in the selected three villages.

Class Stratification in the three Villages

As already stated, till the thirties of this century, class stratification in the three villages used to superimpose over caste stratification. The Nairs who constituted the upper caste came to occupy the upper class position. Both the Nadars and Pulayas constituted the lower class who had no share in the land wealth. But the Nair landlords were numerically small belonging to only a few families. Consequently, there arose the necessity for them to employ a few intermediaries to supervise the agricultural operations. Thus emerged a section among Nadars who initially were employed by Nairs to supervise the agricultural operations. Gradually, some of the landlords entrusted the cultivation to be carried out by the Nadar intermediaries as tenants. The tenancy system was mostly prevalent in Vavara and Kollal villages. As a consequence of this, large tracts of land in Kollal and Vavara villages came to be cultivated by Nadar tenants. They were to give half the yield to the Nair landlords and they had to meet the cost of cultivation and derive profits from the remaining half.

Though this arrangement did not give the tenants any part in the ownership over the land and did not contribute

substantially to their economic prosperity, yet it gave this section of Nadars a higher socio-economic status compared to the Pulayas and other wage labour among Nadars. As the Nairs were the traditional upper class and their exclusive ownership over the land wealth prevented them from pre-occupying themselves with any commercial or business pursuits, the Nair landlords in Kollal and Vavara villages came to be almost exclusively dependant on the rent accuring from their land. On the other hand, when the Nadar tenants came to realise that they could also improve their socio-economic status by acquiring wealth were soon to take up commercial and business pursuits for augmenting their income. By the time of political Independence, a section of Nadars in Vavara and Kollal villages became almost as prosperous as their Nair landlords. Soon after Independence, the economic security of Nairs on account of their land wealth sustained a severe blow when land legislations were enacted. These legislations protected the interests of tenants as against the landlords. Consequently fair rents were fixed for lands. But the fair rent thus fixed were mostly symbolic in nature, and hence the income of landlords became negligible. This, in effect, gave not only the control but also ownership over more land to the Nadar tenants. Thus in Vavara and Kollal villages bulk of land were taken over by Nadar tenants. This process was nearly total in Kollal village reducing all the Nairs excepting a few to be economically dependant on the hitherto Nadar tenants. In the Vavara village, some of the Nair landlords were engaged in direct cultivation and as such those few could retain control over their land. But as in Kollal village the rest of the Nair landlords lost their land to Nadar tenants. In Viakkalloor village, the tenancy system was not prevalent and hence the Nairs continued to hold ownership and control over the land.

In all the three villages, the Pulayas constituted the wage labour and there has been very little change in their class status. They not only constituted the lower caste but also the lowest class. In the early days as now, they did not own any land whatsoever and they used to live in small huts on land which belonged to Nair lords. They were more semi-slaves

than free men. They used to be attached to Nair landlords. When Nadars got ownership and control over lands in Kollal and Vavara villages, Pulayas shifted their allegiance from Nairs to Nadars in these villages. Thus, in these villages, most of the Pulayas who were hitherto attached to Nair landlords came under the control of Nadars. Apart from these shifting allegiance, the class status of Pulayas remained static.

Class Categories

As far as the three villages are concerned, class stratification is essentially dichotomic. By and large people in these villages can be divided into two classes of upper and lower. But the villagers themselves visualize a trichotomic class division of upper, middle and lower. It is found that they include all those who are engaged in manual labour in lower class and income of those in lower class is considered to be below Rupees Two Hundred (Rs. 200). The division between upper class and middle class seems to be superficial than real. They are found to include all those who do not resort to manual labour under the categories of middle and upper classes. But they seem to draw a distinction between upper and middle on the basis of income alone. Middle class is found to be those peasants and a few businessmen who have a monthly income of Rs. 200 to Rs. 300. The upper class are believed to be those having an income of Rs. 300 and above a month.

Interestingly the lower classes are constituted by Nadars and Pulayas in Viakkalloor village, a section of Nadars, a section of Nairs and Pulayas in Vavara village and by the Nairs, Pulayas and a section of Nadars in Kollal village. This distribution indicates that with the changing distribution pattern of scarce values, there tends to be corresponding change in the social stratification.

It is on the basis of income and caste that the villagers draw the class distinction. They give great importance for wealth and income as determining factors behind upper class positions. In the traditional society, both caste and wealth were the basis for determining class positions Both used to

TABLE 18

Number of Class Categories : Villagers' Classification[5]

Castes	*Villagers' Classification of Class Categories*			Total
	Four Categories	*Three Categories*	*Two Categories*	
Nairs	9 (12.16%)	43 (58 12%)	22 (29 72%)	74 (100%)
Nadars	17 (15.04%)	68 (60.18%)	28 (24.78%)	113 (100%)
Pulayas	12 (20%)	35 (58.33%)	13 (21.67%)	60 (100%)
Total	38 (15.37%)	146 (59.12%)	63 (25.51%)	247 (100%)

$X^2 = 2.2771$ $X^2_{.99\,(4)} = 13.28$ Not significant at 1% level.

TABLE 19

Class Background of Villagers : Self-rating[6]

Castes	*Class Categories*				*Total*
	Upper Class	*Middle Class*	*Lower Middle Class*	*Lower Class*	
Nairs	13 (17.57%)	38 (51.36%)	1 (1.35%)	22 (29.72%)	74 (100%)
Nadars	9 (7.96%)	30 (26.55%)	2 (1.78%)	72 (63.71%)	113 (100%)
Pulayas	—	2 (3.34%)	1 (1.67%)	57 (94.99%)	60 (100%)
Total	22 (8.91%)	70 (28.34%)	4 (1.62%)	151 (61.13%)	247 (100%)

X^2—56.7044 $X^2_{.99(8)} = 20.09$ Significant at 1% level.

synchronise. The Nairs who owned the entire land wealth constituted the highest caste in the three villages. Consequently the tendency among the villagers was to include Nairs under upper class sections. When many Nairs lost ownership of their land to Nadars in Kollal and Vavara villages, they had to become agricultural wage labour like the poorest sections among Nadars and Pulayas. Consequently, by the time of political Independence, Upper Caste Status ceased to be an important criteria for upper class position. In Vavara and Kollal villages, when the Nadar tenants became owners of land, they could exercise control and influence over the wage labour among Nadars and Pulayas. Also those sections among Nairs who became wage labour with the loss of their land became dependant on Nadars who became affluent. This situation further reduced the importance of caste as a determining factor in class stratification. Wealth and income provided the richest section among the villagers with influence and power and hence wealth and income by themselves became the most important determining factors in class stratification. In the Viakkalloor village, even though there is no shift in the class positions of Nairs, caste by itself ceased to be conceived as a factor that determines the class position.

An upper class positions used to superimpose over upper caste positions over centuries before Independence, it was the upper caste position that used to be considered as an important attribute of upper class position. When the ownership over land wealth in Vavara and Kollal villages ceased to be the exclusive preserve of upper caste Nairs and when the hitherto lower caste Nadars came to own the land wealth, villagers came to realise the importance of wealth and income in determining the higher socio-economic position in the villages. It is this that is reflected when all the villagers believe that income and wealth constitute the most important determining factor for holding upper class positions in the villages. At present villagers do not consider caste as a significant factor in determining upper class position. Only very few give even secondary importance to caste. For the upper class sections in the village, family background and political power are important factors in determining upper class positions in the villages.

TABLE 20
Important Characteristics of Upper Class Position[7]
(Caste-Wise)

Caste	*Income*	*Caste*	*Political power*	*Religious belief*	*Family background*	*Others*	*Total*
Nairs	54	6	1	3	8	2	74
	(72.98%)	(8.12%)	(1.35%)	(3.93%)	(10.82%)	(2.8%)	(100%)
Nadars	86	12	3	2	10	–	113
	(76.10%)	(10.62%)	(2.65%)	(1.78%)	(8 85%)		(100%)
Pulayas	45	1	1	–	13	–	60
	(74.99%)	(1.67%)	(1.67%)		(21.67%)		(100%)
Total	185	19	5	5	31	2	247
	(74.91%)	(7.69%)	(2.02%)	(2.02%)	(12·55%)	(0.8%)	(100%)

$X^2 = 15.9259$ $X^2_{.99\ (10)} = 23.21$ Not significant at 1% level.

TABLE 21

Important Characteristics of Upper Class Position

(Class-Wise)

Class	*Income*	*Caste*	*Political power*	*Religious belief*	*Family background*	*Others*	*Total*
Upper	40 (83.35%)	4 (8.33%)	–	1 (2.07%)	3 (6.25%)	–	48 (100%)
Lower	144 (72.36%)	14 (7.03%)	5 (2.51%)	4 (2·01%)	29 (14 58%)	3 (1.51%)	199 (100%)
Total	184 (74.49%)	18 (7.29%)	5 (2.02%)	5 (2.02%)	32 (12.95%)	3 (1.22%)	247 (100%)

$X^2_5 = 3.5833$ $X^2_{.99\,(5)} = 15.09$ Not significant at 1% level.

Moreover it is mostly the upper caste Nairs and the upper class section among Nadars who give greater importance to caste and family background compared to wage labour among Nadars and Pulayas.

Changing Pattern of Class Stratification

The drastic changes that have been taking place in the distribution pattern of scarce values of land in the three villages can be seen through the changing class status of family through the preceding three generations. When great grand parents of Nair respondents were almost exclusively from upper class section, a section of the grand parents came down to middle class position. And by the time of previous generation, *i.e.*, parents, many are found to be reduced to the lower class status (Tables 21, 22 and 23). On the other hand, as far as the Nadars are concerned, when all their great grand parents were categorized as lower class, by the time of grand parents, a section of them are elevated to middle class position. By the time of immediately preceding generations, quite a sizeable section of Nadars are shifted to upper class position. The stagnation of the socio-economic status of Pulayas can be seen in their categorization as lower classes all through the generations without practically any change.

The growing discrepancies between the traditional caste stratification and the mergent class stratification are seen more pronouncedly in Vavara and Kollal villages. In the early days there were none among the upper caste Nairs who lived in rented or leased houses. All of them had their own houses. Again, in the early days, in all the three villages the Nadars and the Pulayas used to live in houses or huts, which belonged to Nair land-lords. None of them had either their own land or their own houses. But the situation has considerably changed in Vavara and Kollal villages, also a certain extent in Viakkalloor village. In the Kollal village there is a sizeable section among Nadars who own their houses. Also a section of Nairs now live either in rented or leased houses which belong to Nadar agriculturists. In the Vavara village also the same pattern is found. Only in Viakkalloor village, all the Nairs

TABLE 21A
Class Background of Great Grand Parents[9]

Castes	Class Categories					Total
	Upper	*Upper Middle*	*Middle*	*Lower Middle*	*Lower*	
Nairs	48 (64.86%)	26 (35.14%)	—	—	—	74 (100%)
Nadars	—	—	—	10 (8.85%)	103 (91.15%)	113 (100%)
Pulayas	—	—	—	—	60 (100%)	60 (100%)
Total	48 (19.43%)	26 (10.53%)	—	10 (4.05%)	163 (66.00%)	247 (100%)

$X^2 = 138.5757$ $\quad X^2_{.99\,(10)} = 23.21$ $\quad$ Significant at 1% level.

TABLE 22

Class Background of Grand Parents[10]

Castes	*Class Categories*					*Total*
	Upper	*Upper Middle*	*Middle*	*Lower Middle*	*Lower*	
Nairs	15 (20.27%)	10 (13.51%)	35 (47.31%)	10 (13.51%)	4 (5.40%)	74 (100%)
Nadars	–	–	18 (15.93%)	12 (10.62%)	83 (73.45%)	113 (100%)
Pulayas	–	–	–	2 (3.34%)	58 (96.66%)	60 (100%)
Total	15 (6.07%)	10 (4.05%)	53 (21.46%)	24 (9.72%)	145 (58.70%)	247 (100%)

$X^2 = 120.5882$ $X^2_{.99\,(10)} = 23.21$ Significant at 1% level.

TABLE 23

Class Background of Parents[11]

Castes	Class Categories					Total
	Upper	*Upper Middle*	*Middle*	*Lower Middle*	*Lower*	
Nairs	11 (14.86%)	10 (13.52%)	16 (21.62%)	18 (24.32%)	19 (25.68%)	74 (100%)
Nadars	4 (3.54%)	1 (0.88%)	15 (13.28%)	10 (8.85%)	83 (73.45%)	113 (100%)
Pulayas	–	–	–	5 (8.33%)	55 (91.67%)	60 (100%)
Total	15 (6.07%)	11 (4.45%)	31 (12.55%)	33 (13.37%)	157 (63.56%)	247 (100%)

$X^2 = 66.3459$ $X^2_{.99\ (10)} = 23.21$ Significant at 1% level.

are found to live in their own houses as in the traditional times. But, here again, there are a few Nadar families who came to own land and houses. It is the changing class stratification and the upward mobility among the Nadars that are reflected, when it is found that while most of the Nairs have inherited their houses (79.45 per cent) in the case of Nadars, the houses are mostly acquired ones (82.15 per cent). In the case of land property also, it is found that, in the case of Nairs, they have been progressively loosing control and ownership over land during the preceding three generations. In the case of Nadars, while they did not own land during the time of grand parents, they are found to be progressively acquiring ownership over more and more land during the succeeding decades since the time of grand parents. Again, when the Nairs are found to have inherited substantial part of their land wealth, there are many among Nadars who are found to have acquired their land wealth by their own effort. The stagnation in the class status of Pulayas is reflected when all, excepting one, are found to be living in the rented houses of either the Nadars or Nairs. None of them possess land of their own.

Though, in all the three villages, Nairs constituted the upper class during the pre-Independent days, they have yielded their upper class positions to Nadars in the Kollal and Vavara villages. It is this that is revealed when all the respondents from the Kollal village always cited Nadars for the upper class and middle class positions.[12] In the Vavara village when they gave the names of three individuals having upper class positions, two of them are found to be Nadars and only one of them is found to be a Nair. The same pattern is found in the middle class also. For the lower class position in the village, Nadars, Nairs and Pulayas are included.[13] In the Viakkalloor village, all the three individuals cited for upper class positions are Nairs. For the middle class positions, only one Nadar is found to be included.[14] Among the lower class, only Nadars and Pulayas are included.

Villagers belonging to lower class sections of the three villages are found to be reconciled to their poverty. Though they realise that their condition is hopeless, they believe that there is nothing that can be done to improve their economic

status. It is probably this belief on their part that make many of them pessimistic towards future and believe in fate. In this, the traditional religious outlook plays an important role. Their belief in fate is grounded on the belief that the human life is a predestined one and hence man can do nothing to ameliorate his conditions. If he does not revolt against the present system, he would be able to have a better life during the next birth. These traditional religious beliefs were essentially for reinforcing the differential distribution pattern of scarce values. When those who do not own land rely on god and fate, there will be no threat to upper class positions. Though the traditional distribution pattern of scarce values has undergone change, it remains grossly differential as in the old days and probably these beliefs persist for sustaining the persisting differential distribution to scarce values of land. It is probably this that make the lower class to believe that they can never improve their status position. This belief is again mostly confined to Pulayas and the poorer sections among Nadars and Nairs. On the other hand, upper class sections among Nadars and Nairs believe that it is possible for one to improve the status. All the villagers are found to believe that the upper class sections always try to maintain their class positions.

In the traditional society, all those who owned and controlled the scarce values of land constituted not only the upper class, but also the upper castes. In other words, the caste system enabled the upper classes to perpetuate their upper class position.

NOTES

1. W.G. Runciman, "Class, Status and Power" in (J.A. Jackson, "Sociological Studies I: Social Stratification"), 1967, Cambridge University Press, p 23.
2. Bendix and Lipset, "Class, Status and Power : A Reader in Social Stratification", 1953, Free Press of Glenco, pp. 75-76.
3. Charles H. Page, "Social Class and American Sociology" Bendix and Lipset (Eds.), *op. cit.*, p. 48.
4. Pitrim A. Sorokin, "What is a Social Class" in (Bendix and Lipset Eds.) *op. cit.*, pp. 87 and 88.
5. Appendix I, Q II-1,

6. *Ibid.*, Q. II-2.
7. *Ibid.*, Q. II-6.
8. *Ibid.*
9. *Ibid.*, Q. II-3 (*iii*).
10. *Ibid.*, Q. II-3 (*ii*).
11. *Ibid.*, Q. II-3 (*i*).
12. *Ibid.*, Q. II-5 and V. 6.
13. *Ibid.*
14. *Ibid.*

CHAPTER SEVEN

INTRA-CLASS AND INTER-CLASS RELATIONS

Class is a new phenomenon in India. In traditional society, caste played the role of class and the upper castes occupied the position of upper class, and the lower castes constituted the lower class.

The difference between caste and class is that, inter-caste relations were comparatively more harmonious than inter-class relations. "Classes in contradistinction, form segmentary stratification, when various strata or segments are motivated by a feeling of competition rather than that of co-operation as obtained in caste".[1]

Social activities of people are mainly limited within each class. Though some times, the upper class people may have to depend on lower classes for various services,[2] these people are kept at a distance. Upper classes invite, for various social functions like marriage, only those people who have the same status. This is true in the case of lower classes also. Even for marital relationships, people prefer a person of their own class because of the fear that, some times they have to confront 'social uncertainty, acculturation and over conformity'.[3]

Economic activities go beyond one's own class. If economic interactions are confined within the class, "then the rise in its socio-economic status will be retarded and its socio-economic

status tends to become inferior to that of the opposing group".[4]

As in the case of economic interactions, political activities are also not limited to each class. In political field no one group can win alone, and hence inter-relations are greater here. Also often competition may be between persons belonging to the same class and the competitors seek the help of people from other classes.

Intra-Class Relations

It was the upper caste Nairs who functioned as the upper class. As all others in the three villages were agricultural wage labour, they together formed the lower class. But they did not form a well knit group because of the differences in the nature of their work. Some of them were palm tree tappers, and also labour supervisors under the Nair landlords. As a consequence of this, though they were economically as poor as the rest of the wage labour, they constituted a distinctive group, which, in course of time, came to be designated as Nadars. The unskilled agricultural wage labour class continued to be a distinct class category. They also, in course of time, became a distinct caste group called Pulayas. As the class division synchronized with the caste division, the intra-caste and the inter-caste relations were more or less same as the intra-class and inter-class relations.

When a section of the Nadars in Vavara and Kollal villages became land proprietors and thereby raised their class status, the inter-class and intra-class relations in Vavara and Kollal villages assumed new dimensions. The intra-class relations after political Independence came to enfold the upper class sections, both among Nadars and Nairs. Till early thirties, the inter-class relations were same as the inter-caste relations. Now a section of Nadars are also elevated to upper class positions while a section of Nairs are reduced to lower class positions.

As a consequence of this, interactions within the upper class include the upper class sections among both Nadars and

Nairs. But such inter-caste interactions are not many among the lower class comprising Nair, Nadar and Pulaya agricultural wage labour.

In social, political and educational life of the three villages, interactions are assuming more and more class orientation rather than caste orientation. During pre-Independent days, as class and caste super-imposed over each other, it was caste oriented interaction that could be found in all these sectors.

But when a section of Nadars elevated themselves to upper class position in Kollal and Vavara villages, caste orientation has been gradually replaced by class orientation with regard to social, educational and political activities. Consequently it is possible to find very close relations between upper class Nadars and Nairs in the socio-political life of Kollal and Vavara villages. In marriage and other social functions upper class Nairs invite the affluent Nadars and the latter also reciprocate. Such class based interactions are more manifest in the political activities. In the Panchayat elections, though caste continues to be a crucial factor class, also plays an important role. The representatives of the three villages in the Panchayat belong to the upper class section among Nadars and Nairs. When two upper class Nadars are representing the Kollal and Vavara villages, it is an upper class Nair who is representing the Viakkalloor village. The upper class sections in all the three villages are found to prefer only a person with the upper class background to be the president of the Panchayat. On the other hand the lower class sections are found to aspire to make a person of their own background as the president of the Panchayat. At the same time, there are a few among the lower classes who are found to favour a person with upper class background to head the Panchayat and to represent the constituency. Most of those from the lower class who, thus give support to the upper class, are found to be the lower class Nairs. This is, probably, because the lower class sections among Nairs were, till recently, the landlords and the upper class. Therefore, even though they are reduced to lower class status, yet, they may still be retaining

their upper class orientations and values. Their caste based kinship relations with other upper class Nairs serve to provide the necessary realism for their identification with the upper classes. Such upper class identification is also found among a few lower class Nadars and Pulayas. This is probably due to their anxiety to enhance their socio-economic status. Class background is found to influence neighbourhood relations and personal relationships. The upper class sections in all the three villages were found to prefer only those of their own status in the neighbourhood except in the case of a few Nadars and Nairs. The lower class sections, on the whole, are found to favour persons of their own economic status as neighbours. The class behaviour is more marked in the case of personal friendship. The close personal relationship is found to be confined to one's own class only. For marital relationship, when all those who belong to upper class section are found to prefer persons of their class, a good section of the lower class are also found to prefer persons with upper class background. This also is probably due to the anxiety to improve the economic status among a few from the lower classes. In all these, greater identification of upper class is found among the Nair upper classes compared to Nadars and Pulayas.

Inter-Class Relations

Till the rise of a section of Nadars to upper class positions, the inter-class relations super-imposed over inter-caste relations. In social, political and cultural fields the Nair upper class always kept aloof from lower class Nadars and Pulayas. There was practically no interaction between Nairs and other caste groups. As there was no inter-caste mobility, inter-class mobility was also not possible. The social distance practices came handy for Nairs for keeping Nadars and Pulayas in their subordinate positions As the inter-caste relations had religious approval and sanctions which necessitated voluntary superordinate-subordinate relations, the inter-class relations also were never strained and conflicting. When the traditional caste system disintegrated with political Independence and subsequent reform legislations, inter-caste relations became more and more conflicting and strained. This naturally has reflected in the rela-

tions between those upper caste Nairs who retained upper class positions and the lower class sections of Nadars and Pulayas. When a section of Nadars got upper class position in Vavara and Kollal villages, they came closer to upper class Nairs while retaining their caste relations with the lower class section of their own caste.

Under the traditional caste system, the upper caste Nairs used to consider both Nadars and Pulayas not only as inferior to them but also as dependant on them. All their dealings with Nadars and Pulayas were characterised by this super-ordinate-subordinate relationship. This was possible because they were not only the upper caste but also the upper class. But the disintegration of caste system and the loss of Nair monopoly over land wealth brought about radical changes in their relationship with other castes. Bulk of the Nairs in Kollal village and nearly half of them in Vavara village lost their ownership over land and became economically dependant on Nadars who emerged as land proprietors during post-Independent period. As a consequence to this, those Nairs who are reduced to the status of wage labour, now no more consider the Nadars and Pulayas as inferior and dependant on them. The super-ordinate-subordinate relationships now no more synchronize with the upper caste-lower caste relationships. The different sections among Nadars in Kollal and Vavara villages consider the agricultural wage labour among their own community and also those among Pulayas and Nairs as inferior and economically dependant on them. Thus both Nairs and Nadars who belong to upper class in three villages consider others as inferior to them.

As far as the Nadars and Pulayas were concerned they used to consider themselves as inferior to upper class Nairs in the traditional society. But this caste based feeling of inferiority has ceased to be any more relevant now. Now such inferiority feeling is mostly on the basis of class positions. Not only the Nadars and Pulayas, but also a section of Nairs who have become the wage labour are found to consider themselves as inferior to the upper class Nadars and Nairs.

TABLE 24

Social Distance Between Upper and Lower Classes[5]

Class	Social distance is kept				Social distance is not kept				Total
	Nairs	Nadars	Pulayas	Total	Nairs	Nadars	Pulayas	Total	
Upper	17 (50.00%)	17 (50.00%)	—	34 (100%)	12 (85.72%)	2 (14.28%)	—	14 (100%)	48
Lower	31 (25 00%)	65 (52.42%)	28 (22.58%)	124 (100%)	14 (18.67%)	29 (38.67%)	32 (42.67%)	75 (100%)	199
Total	48 (30.38%)	82 (51.89%)	28 (17.73%)	158 (100%)	26 (29.22%)	31 (34.84%)	32 (35.94%)	89 (100%)	247

$X^2 = 7.1598$ $X^2_{.99(2)} = 9.21$ Not significant at 1% level.

$X^2 = 7.1598$ $X^2_{.95(2)} = 5.98$ Significant at 1% level.

$X^2_2 = 21.2265$ $X^2_{.99(2)} = 9.21$ Significant at 1% level.

TABLE 25

Concept of Upper Class[6]

Class	*Vicious*	*Unscrupulous*	*God fearing*	*Religious minded*	*Helping*	*Philan-thropic*	*Stingy*	*Others*	*Total*
Upper	4 (8.33%)	3 (6.25%)	20 (41.67%)	15 (31.25%)	6 (12 50%)	–	–	–	48 (100%)
Lower	66 (33.17%)	39 (19.61%)	10 (5.03%)	5 (2.51%)	6 (3.01%)	4 (2.01%)	69 (34.66%)	– –	199 (100%)
Total	70 (28 34%)	42 (17.00%)	30 (12.14%)	20 (8.10%)	12 (4.86%)	4 (1.62%)	69 (27.94%)	–	247 (100%)

$X^2_6 = 97.5667$ $X^2_{.99(6)} = 16.81$ Significant at 1% level.

TABLE 26
Concept of Lower Class[7]

Class	*Contemptible*	*Unscrupulous*	*Vicious*	*God fearing*	*Religious minded*	*Helping*	*Philan-thropic*	*Others*	*Total*
Upper	3 (6.26%)	14 (29.18%)	15 (31.26%)	2 (4.16%)	2 (4.16%)	4 (8.33%)	1 (2.07%)	7 (14.58%)	48 (100%)
Lower	2 (1.00%)	4 (2.01%)	3 (1.51%)	68 (34.18%)	53 (26.63%)	33 (16.58%)	36 (18.09%)	–	199 (100%)
Total	5 (2.02%)	18 (7.29%)	18 (7.29%)	70 (28.34%)	55 (22.27%)	37 (14.64%)	37 (14.64%)	7 (6.88%)	247 (100%)

$X^2_7 = 155.7013$ $X^2_{.99\,(7)} = 18.48$ Very significant at 1% level.

In social life in the three villages, though the interactions are to a certain extent even now are based on caste affiliations, yet among the upper classes, class also plays an important role. In most of the social functions like marriage the upper caste Nairs in all the three villages are found to invite the affluent sections among the Nadars also. As such extra caste participation is confined to upper class sections alone, it can be said that social interactions are more and more assuming class characteristics, while the caste characteristics are on the way out. Now the interaction in social life between the upper class and lower class sections of the three villages are quite minimal and mostly confined to Nairs alone. This is because the lower class among Nairs were hitherto the upper classes and as such possess certain kinship relations with those Nairs who still remain as upper classes. It is found that both the upper and the lower classes keep social distance from each other.

The social gulf between the upper classes and the lower classes can be seen in the image which each class has about the other. When the upper classes consider themselves as God-fearing, religious minded, philanthropic etc., they consider the lower classes as contemptible, unscrupulous, vicious etc. Similarly the lower classes consider upper classes as vicious, stingy and unscrupulous while they consider themselves as God-fearing, philanthropic, religious minded etc.

The class preference is found in the political activities and intimate social relationships. Both the lower classes and upper classes prefer only members of their own classes to represent them in the Panchayat and legislative assemblies and similar preferences also have been shown as to the neighbourhood relationships and personal friendship. For marital relationships, when the upper classes prefer only their own classes, there are a few among the lower classes who prefer upper classes.

NOTES

1. Yogendra Singh, "Caste and Class : Some aspects of Continuity and Change", Sociological Bulletin, Vol. XXII, September, 1968, No. 2. p. 168.

2. Dan A. Chekki, "Social Stratification and Trends of Social Mobility in Modern Urban India", The Indian Journal of Social Work, Vol. XXXI, January 1971, No 4, p. 371.

3. Peter Blau, "Social Mobility and Interpersonal relations", American Sociological Review 21, June 1950, p. 209.

4. G. Ramachandra Raj, "Functions and Dysfunctions of Social Conflict", Popular Prakashan, Bombay, 1974, p. 170.

5. *Ibid.*, Q. II-9 (a).

6. *Ibid* , Q. II-14.

7. *Ibid.*, Q. II-15.

CHAPTER EIGHT

CHANGING PATTERN OF SECTARIAN AND CASTE STRATIFICATION AND CHANGING PATTERN OF POLITICAL RELATIONS

Caste and Class Stratification and Leadership

As caste and class superimpose over each other in the three villages before political Independence, political power and political leadership also used to conform to caste and class stratification. The Nairs who constituted the upper class and upper caste provided the political leadership. In all the three villages, the Karanavar or Head of the richest Nair family used to be the village Chief. The Nair, Chieftains used to be vested with the administrative and political control. The disputes among the villagers, irrespective of their class background, used to be referred to these chieftains for settlement and the awards given by them for such disputes were final. Any challenge to Nair propriety over land wealth from either Nadars or Pulayas used to be severely dealt with. Also violation of social distance practices like untouchability used to be curbed by the Nair chiefs. The political authority of Nair Chieftains had necessary legitimisation, as their authority (of Nair) had the approval from the Maharajas of Travancore. In return for such approval, it was the obligation of the chieftains to supply means and arms for the Maharajahs at the time of war. Also they had to maintain Kalaries for training men in the use of arms. But the

militia used to be composed of exclusively by Nairs. Nadars and Pulayas were never given any opportunity for getting any training in the use of arms. They were also strictly prohibited from using and carrying arms.

The exclusive political power of Nairs enabled them to keep Nadars and Pulayas in subservient and subordinate positions. This traditional pattern of political leadership in which caste and class background played the most crucial role has undergone considerable change when the class stratification in the villages changed. When the land ownership shifted from Nairs to Nadars in Vavara and Kollal villages, a section of Nadars also got themselves elevated to upper class positions. Again the political Independence gave more emphasis on numerical support for determining political leadership.

Under the traditional caste stratification, where class and caste synchronize, political leadership tends to be vested numerically smaller upper castes. Political authority tends to be used for curbing any challenge to the economic interests of the upper caste from the numerically larger lower castes. But, when the traditional class stratification changes by inducting a section of the lower castes to the upper class, the political authority ceases to be the exclusive preserve of the upper castes. Under the circumstances, political leadership tends to be determined by class status and numerical support. Also, caste ceases to be the major determining factor behind leadership. In other words, when caste and class stratification do not synchronize, political leadership tends to be determined by class status rather than caste status.

Class Status and Leadership

As the emergent land proprietors among Nadars effectively controlled the political behaviour of Nadars in Vavara village and Kollal village, they emerged as powerful leaders in the two villages replacing the traditional Nair leadership. But in the Viakkalloor village, where the Nairs still retain ownership and control over land, they continue to wield political power also.

The post-Independence changes, in the political administration have brought about an end to the traditional inherited political power of Nairs in this region. This has resulted in considerable reduction of their influence in these villages also. When Nairs have literally lost their control over the land to Nadars in the Kollal village, they simultaneously lost their political status also. Consequently the political power in this village is exclusively vested on the newly emergent Nadar land proprietors. In other words political leadership is vested on the Nadar upper class section in the village. The representative of Panchayat in this village is the richest Nadar agriculturist. As a section of Nairs, Pulayas and the bulk of Nadars in this village constituted the agriculture wage labour, they do not have any place in the political leadership.

In the Vavara village, land ownership is evenly divided between Nadars and Nairs and, as such, both Nadars and Nairs figure among the political leaders. But, at the same time as the Nadars are numerically superior, the Panchayat member from this village is also a Nadar. He is a rich landlord belonging to the upper class section among Nadars. Here also political leadership synchronizes with economic leadership. All those who figure as leaders both among Nadars and Nairs belong to upper class section. There are none from agriculture wage labour.

In the Viakkalloor village, there is very little change in the traditional pattern of ownership over land wealth. The entire land wealth in this village is owned by a few Nair families. Though during pre-Independent days, Nair landlords had absolute control over Nadars and Pulayas, they, after political Independence, no more wield so much political power. Nairs continue to retain the political leadership of the village. The Panchayat member of this village is a Nair who is also an agriculturist.

In the Kollal village, the upper class Nadars not only provided leadership in political sphere but also in economic, educational and social spheres as well. It is also found that influential economic leaders wield considerable influence in the

political field also. It is they who are again found to be influential in social and educational spheres. In Kollal village all such leaders are Nadars.

In the Vavara village, the economic leadership is evenly divided between upper class sections of both Nadars and Nairs. They also provide political, educational and social leadership.

As far as the Viakkalloor village is concerned, it is the upper class Nairs who provide leadership in political, social and educational spheres.

In all the three villages, Pulayas do not have any share in the political leadership. Among the influential leaders sighted by the respondents, there are no Pulayas. In the economic, educational and social spheres also, there are none among the Pulayas who are considered as leaders.

The upper class section in all the three villages prefer those of the same status in holding political offices. At the same time, the lower class section prefers a representative of a lower class background to represent their Panchayat and Assembly constituencies. Though such preferences are shown by all the villagers, when it comes to casting their votes, they give their votes to those having an upper class background. It is always those having upper class background who are found to secure majority of votes in all the three villages. This is because, along with class preferences, caste and sectarian preferences are also found among the villagers. The Nairs, Nadars and Pulayas prefer members of their respective castes to represent Panchayat and Assembly constituencies. As the richest section in each caste can command the support of others, it is the upper class section who always got elected to the Panchayat and Assembly constituencies.

In other words, caste and sectarian preferences in elections are only secondary to class influences. The elections of upper class Nadar and Nair representatives to the Panchayat and an upper class Nadar representative to the constituency show that

class is the decisive basis in determining political leadership as far as the three villages are concerned.

The elections of Panchayat and Assembly constituencies are always fought on the basis of caste. Nairs, Nadars and Pulayas in the three villages are found to extend their political support on the basis of caste. As the political leaders among Nairs and Nadars are from upper classes, it is they who invariably derive such political support from their respective caste members. Consequently the agricultural wage labour among both Nadars and Nairs extend their political support to agriculturists among these two castes.

TABLE 27

Help to Caste Members When Need Arises in Political Field[1]

(Caste-wise)

Castes	*Help extended to caste members*	*No caste consideration*	*Total*
Nairs	48 (64.86%)	26 (35.14%)	74 (100%)
Nadars	81 (71.68%)	32 (28.32%)	113 (100%)
Pulayas	45 (75%)	15 (25%)	60 (100%)
Total	174 (70.44%)	73 (29.56%)	247 (100%)

$X^2_2 = 1.7717$ $X^2_{.99(2)} = 9\ 21$ Not significant at 1% level.

TABLE 28

Help to Caste Members When Need Arises in Political Field[2]

(Class-wise)

Class	*Help extended to caste members*	*No caste consideration*	*Total*
Upper	33 (68.75%)	15 (31.25%)	48 (100%)
Lower	141 (70 84%)	58 (29.16%)	199 (100%)
Total	174 (70.44%)	73 (29.56%)	247 (100%)

Determinants of Leadership

As already pointed out the leadership in each caste is based on the economic background of the leaders. The high income and wealth are considered as the most significant factors in the caste leadership. The political leaders in all the three villages belong to the upper class sections among Nadars and Nairs. In other words, political leadership in all the three villages is vested on only the upper class sections.

Even though political leadership is vested on the upper class, caste continues to play a role in determining the leadership. This is evident in the way in which villagers exercise their franchise in elections. Since Independence, all the candidates for elections to Panchayat and Assembly constituencies from this area, belonged to upper class sections and in choosing from among them, it was the caste or the sectarian background that was taken into consideration by the villagers. As the Pulayas never contested the elections, they have been exercising their franchise mostly on the basis of their economic dependance on the upper class section in each village. Those who are dependant on Nair agriculturists favour those candidates supported by them. Similarly those who are dependant on Nadar agriculturists favour those who are supported by Nadars. In the case of Nairs and Nadars, most of them are found to favour candidates belonging to their respective castes. At the same time, it may be noted that irrespective of their caste affiliations, all the candidates belong to upper class section. Thus, it can be seen that when class background being the same, it is the sectarian background that determines the nature of political behaviour.

TABLE 29

Essential Pre-Requisites of A Caste Leader[3]

Castes	*Income*	*Religion*	*Family*	*Political ower*	*Occupation*	*Others*	*Total*
Nairs	37 (50%)	–	24 (32.44%)	11 (14.86%)	—	2 (2.70%)	74 (100%)
Nadars	61 (54.40%)	10 (8.85%)	20 (17.70%)	19 (16.40%)	–	3 (2.65%)	113 (100%)
Pulayas	37 (61.67%)	5 (8.33%)	8 (13.33%)	1 (1.67%)	3 (5%)	6 (10%)	60 (100%)
Total	135 (54.65%)	15 (6.07%)	52 (21.05%)	31 (12.55%)	3 (1.22%)	11 (4.46%)	247 (100%)

$X^2_{10} = 34.6151$ $X^2_{.99\,(10)} = 23.21$ Significant at 1% level.

TABLE 30

Caste Considerations and the Nature of Voting During Elections[4]

(Caste-wise)

Castes	*Caste affiliation is taken into consideration in voting*	*Caste affiliation is not taken into consideration in voting*	*Total*
Nairs	53 (71.62%)	21 (28.38%)	74 (100%)
Nadars	78 (69.03%)	35 (30.97%)	113 (100%)
Pulayas	42 (70%)	18 (30%)	60 (100%)
Total	173 (70.04%)	74 (29.96%)	247 (100%)

$X^2_2 = 1.6706$ $X^2_{.99(2)} = 9.21$ Not significant at 1% level.

TABLE 31

Caste Considerations and the Nature of Voting During Elections[5]

(Class-wise)

Class	*Caste affiliation is taken into consideration in voting*	*Caste affiliation is not taken into consideration in voting*	*Total*
Upper	35 (72.93%)	13 (27.07%)	48 (100%)
Lower	138 (69.35%)	61 (30.65%)	199 (100%)
Total	173 (70.04%)	74 (29.96%)	247 (100%)

Moreover, it is agreed by all that the influential persons, in the villages belong to upper class sections. It is also realized by all that the basis of power which influential leaders possess are due to their upper class position. Along with this, their influence among their respective caste is also considered to be an important factor which determines their influence in the village as a whole.

Among the influential leaders recognized by village leaders, there are none from the Pulayas. This is, probably, because the Pulayas in the three villages belong to the lower class

section. In the Kollal village, most of the influential persons are Nadars. In Vavara, the upper and middle class sections among Nadars hold influential position. In the Viakkalloor village all the influential persons are Nairs and there are none among Nadars and Pulayas.

Dravida Munnetta Kazhagam (DMK) is found to have the largest fallowing in the three villages. Majority of Nairs and Nadars extend their support to this party. But in the case of Pulayas, only a small section among them is found to be in favour of it. Congress Organization is the other party commanding the support of a sizeable section of the villagers. Quite a large section of Nadars and majority of Pulayas are supporting this party. As far as the Nairs are concerned, support for Congress Organization comes only from a small section among them. The Communist Party of India (Marxist) also has a small fallowing in the three villages. The support for them comes mostly from the Pulayas. There are also a few Nairs who are found to be supporting the Communist Party (Marxist).

As far as the upper class sections among Nairs and Nadars are concerned, most of them extend their support to the ruling D.M.K. Among them there is only a very small section supporting Congress Organization. In other words, the upper classes are with the ruling party. Those few who are found to be with the Congress Organization are invested with the leadership of the party in the three villages. Similarly the leadership of the ruling DMK is also with the upper classes.

The substantial support to the Congress Organization comes from the lower classes. It is the agricultural wage labour among the lower classes who are found to be supporting Communist Party (Marxist). But the strength of the party compared to the other two parties is negligible.

The villagers are found to be supporting the political parties on the basis of their caste and class affiliations. As far as the upper classes are concerned, it is essentially the class considerations that determine the political behaviour. Caste is also an

important factor. As a whole, ideological considerations have no place in the political behaviour of upper classes. But, among the lower classes, there is a sizeable section who support the political party on the basis of ideological considerations But, among them also, majority are influenced by caste and class considerations in their political behaviour. Compared to Nairs and Nadars, it is the Pulayas who are found to be taking ideology as a consideration in their political affiliation. All those who are motivated by ideological consideration among Pulayas are found to be supporting the Communist Party (Marxist)

As far as the upper class sections are concerned, the nature of their political affiliations is found to be dependant on the extent to which they can safeguard their economic interests through political power. That is why the upper classes in the villages have shifted their support to the ruling D.M.K. from the Congress when the latter lost political power in the state. A similar change in the political affiliations can be seen among a section of the lower classes also. This is because these sections among the lower classes are economically dependant on upper class sections and hence they will have to follow the upper classes in the political sphere. It is the necessity to safeguard the economic interests that is given as the main factor for this shift in the political affiliations.

NOTES

1. *Ibid.*, Q. III-2, (*iii*).
2. *Ibid.*
3. *Ibid.*, Q. III-15.
4. *Ibid.*, Q. III-16.
5. *Ibid.*

CHAPTER NINE

CASTE AND CLASS STRATIFICATION, OCCUPATION AND ECONOMIC LIFE

Traditional Caste and Class Stratification, Occupation and Economic Life

As already stated, the traditional class stratification used to synchronize with traditional caste stratification in all the three villages. Consequently, the occupation and economic life used to conform to this pattern of stratification. The Nairs, who constituted the upper class and upper caste, owned the entire land wealth. Till the beginning of this century, Nairs used to cultivate the land by themselves by using the Nadar and Pulaya labour. But, there were no instances where Nairs themselves cultivated the land by using their own labour. Each joint family used to have a section of Nadar and Pulaya population who owned allegiance to the family concerned. As the cultivation pattern of the village required sustained and uninterrupted supply of labour, such allegiance of Nadar and Pulaya labour was necessary. In return for their labour, Nair landlords used to provide minimum life requirements to the dependant Nadar and Pulaya labourers. The wage was in kind. Apart from the wage, during non-agricultural seasons, the landlords had to provide for the bare minimum necessities of the labourers.

In addition to economic power, Nairs also wielded political power. They used to wear arms and had to serve in Rajahs, army if called upon to do so. Due to these political pre-occupations, the Nair landlords could not devote their entire time for the supervision of agricultural operations. Consequently, a few Nadar families who owned allegiance to their respective landlords were entrusted with supervisory work in all agricultural operations. It was for these supervisors to decide as to how many Nadar and Pulaya labourers would be required to work in the land and what wage should be given to each. Again, it was through these intermediaries, that the landlords used to disburse their aid to the labour during off seasons.

In course of time, these Nadar intermediaries were assigned land to be cultivated on their own. In return, they were to give part of the yield to the landlords. Though they acquired tenancy status when they started their own cultivation, simultaneously they had to supervise the agricultural operations in the land belonging to their landlords. As the landlords could secure more than half the yield through these tenancy arrangements without shouldering any responsibility, most of them in Vavara and Kollal villages leased out bulk of their land to Nadar tenants. Thus, apart from Nair landlords and agriculturists, a section of Nadars also emerged as farmers whose socio-economic status was superior to that of the other Nadars and Pulaya wage labour. Apart from these emergent farmers and a few petty traders among the Nadars, rest of the Nadars and Pulayas constituted the agricultural labour. Therefore, the main occupational roles in the three villages were that of landlords, agriculturists, farmers, petty traders and agricultural wage labour. As the economy in the three villages continues to be agricultural, this pattern of occupation even now persists. Only difference is that, with the various land legislations, the institution of landlordship no more exists. Therefore, the prevalent pattern of occupation in the three villages consists of agriculturists, farmers, petty traders and agricultural wage labour.

Thus is can be said, that the occupational pattern may tend to persist when basic economy of a society continues to be

agricultural. But if the class stratification synchronizes with caste stratification, the occupational pattern tends to conform with the caste stratification. The moment class stratification ceases to superimpose over caste stratification, occupational pattern also ceases to synchronize with caste stratification. On the other hand, occupational pattern tends to conform to the class stratification.

Changing Pattern of Occupational Life

With the abolition of landlordism, a large number of Nadar families, who were hitherto tenants, became owners of land in their own right. At the same time, in Kollal village where the Nair landlords have leased out the bulk of their land to Nadars, they lost their ownership and control over their land to the tenants concerned. When joint family properties were partitioned, individual members of the families secured control and ownership over their respective land share. But they found it difficult to cultivate the land on their own. This was because they did not have any experience or training for the same. Also, when they lost their economic protection which they used to get from the joint families, it became necessary for many of them to sell their land for a living. The lands, thus sold, were bought by the Nadars. This has resulted into a radical redistribution of occupational roles among different castes.

There ceased to be any landlords in the Kollal village. The landlords and agriculturists among the Nairs were reduced to small farmers and agricultural wage labour. On the other hand almost all the Nadar farmers became agriculturists.

In all the three villages those who live in their own houses are either Nairs or Nadars. A section of Nairs live in rented houses in Kollal and Vavara villages (12.16 per cent). All of them are agricultural wage labour who are employed by the Nadar agriculturists in Kollal village and by both Nadar and Nair agriculturists in Vavara village. Similarly the wage labour, among the Nadars and all the Pulayas in three villages are found to be living in rented houses. Only agriculturists and farmers

live in their own houses.

The houses owned by Nadars are acquired or bought either by them or their fathers. None of them are found to be having house which form part of their inheritance. On the other hand houses owned by Nairs are all inherited ones (75.81 per cent).

Again it is the Nadars who owned bulk of the cultivable land in Kollal and Vavara villages. Excepting a few tracts of land, the entire land wealth in Kollal village belong to Nadar agriculturists. In the Vavara village they owned 65 per cent of land wealth. Compared to this there are no Nadar agriculturists in the Viakkalloor village. In this village, the Nair landlords themselves used to cultivate the land and as such there was no tenancy system under which Nadars could secure ownership or control over their land. Even when joint family properties were partitioned, the individual members, who came to own land, could easily carry out cultivation by themselves in their respective land share. Therefore, there was very little alienation of land by Nair landlords or agriculturists and as a consequence to this, excepting a few acres, the entire cultivable land in this village continues to be in the hands of Nairs.

It was found that, during the last three generations, there has been a consistent decline in the economic status of Nairs in Kollal and Vavara villages while it remained more or less static in Viakkalloor village. In the case of those Nairs, who owned land in Vavara and Kollal villages, it was found that the quantum of land holdings of their parents, grand parents and great grand parents were much higher than the present holdings. In this regard, there has been very little change in the land-holdings held by Nairs during the last generations in Viakkalloor village. Compared to Nairs, the land holdings of Nadars in Viakkalloor and Vavara villages is much higher than that of the land owned by their parents and grand parents. Excepting very few cases, the Nadars in the previous generations did not possess any land.[1] When the land properties of all the Nadars are found to be acquired either by them or their parents, such properties are found to be inherited through generations in the case of Nairs. In the case of Pulayas, they do not own any land.

Stratum Degradation and Stratum Upgradation

Along with these changes in the economic background, there has been corresponding changes in the occupational life of the three villages. The changing occupations with the changing economic background is more pronounced in the case of Nairs and Nadars. During the last three generations, when the Nairs alienated their land to Nadars, there has been a down-gradation in their occupational life also. When all the Nairs were land proprietors three generations ago, quite a few among them became farmers at the time of their grand fathers. By the time of previous generation, leaving aside a few, majority of Nairs were reduced to farmers. Even this has changed by contemporary generation. A substantial section among Nairs in the Kollal and Vavara villages suffered further deterioration in the occupational status by becoming agricultural labour.

In the case of Nadars, the process has been just the other way round. When, excepting a few who were tenants and petty traders, all of them were agricultural wage labour, the pattern has altered considerably during the time of their grand parents. By this time, quite a few among Nadars became tenants and among the tenants quite a few became farmers. But this change is confined to Kollal and Vavara villages. During the last generation a few Nadars became agriculturists in Kollal and Vavara villages. Also the number of farmers and tenants among them has considerably gone up. By contemporary generation, the agriculturists in Kollal village are almost exclusively constituted by Nadars. In the Vavara village, majority of agriculturists are again constituted by Nadars. Quite a substantial section among them have become farmers. But in Viakkalloor village, where there has been no change in the economic background of Nairs and Nadars, the occupational pattern also remained more or less the same during the last three generations.

In the case of Pulayas, their occupation continued to be that of agricultural labours. There are none among the Nair agriculturists who have acquired occupational status. All their property holdings are inherited and consequently their

economic status is also inherited. Similarly the Nadar and Pulaya wage labour also had inherited occupational status because, for generations, it is they who constituted the wage labour in the three villages. The farmers among the Nairs and agricultural wage labour among them were all originally landlords and it was, during the course of last three generations, that they came to be reduced to the lower class status which they are holding at present. Though the present occupational statuses which they hold are theoretically acquired ones, they are inferior to the statuses which they hitherto used to hold. This process by which large number of individuals belonging to the higher strata of the society are brought down to lower strata by means of reducing their control and ownership over the scarce values of production and a corresponding down-gradation of the occupational status may be termed as stratum degradation.

In the case of Nadars, this process is found to be on reverse. As far as the Nadars are concerned, the higher occupational status of farmers and agriculturists are found to be acquired ones. All the Nadar agriculturists and farmers are found to have reached the higher status from that of their original status of agricultural wage labour, a few generation ago. This process by which a large number of individuals from the lower strata of the society are elevated to the higher strata by acquiring control and ownership over means of production and a corresponding acquisition of higher economic status may be termed as stratum upgradation.

In the case of Pulayas and a large section of Nadars, there has been no change in the occupational status. They continued to have no control and ownership over the land and are kept as wage labour for generations. This process by which a large section of the society by with-holding from them any control and ownership over the means of production and by forcing them to sell their labour for their sustenance may be termed as stratum maintenance.

Compared to the upper classes, it is among the lower classes that stratum maintenance seems to be more operative.

It is stratum upgradation which seems to be operative among the upper classes.

TABLE 1

Nature of Occupation[2]

(Caste-wise)

Castes	*Hereditary*	*Not hereditary*	*Total*
Nairs	41 (55.42%)	33 (44.58%)	74 (100%)
Nadars	58 (51.33%)	55 (48.67%)	113 (100%)
Pulayas	55 (91.67%)	5 (8.33%)	60 (100%)
Total	154 (62.35%)	93 (37.65%)	247 (100%)

$X^2_2 = 40\ 5527$ $X^2_{.99\,(2)} = 9.21$ Significant at 1% level.

TABLE 2

Nature of Occupation[3]

(Class-wise)

Classes	*Hereditary*	*Not hereditary*	*Total*
Upper	25 (52.08%)	23 (47.92%)	48 (100%)
Lower	129 (64.82%)	70 (35.18%)	199 (100%)
Total	154 (62.35%)	93 (37.65%)	247 (100%)

It may be noted that, with the degeneration of a large number of Nair landlords and agriculturists to that of farmers and agriculture wage labour, the proportion of agriculture wage labour in three villages has considerably gone high while the number of agriculturists comprising both Nadars and Nairs has also come down considerably. On the contrary, as against the traditional dichotomous stratification, there emerged an intermediary strata consisting of farmers.

As these farmers also work in their fields along with agricultural wage labour and their economic condition is not in any way considerably higher than that of wage labour, they cannot be bracketed together as a class which is different from that of wage labour. Nevertheless most of them identify themselves with agriculturists and seldom conscious of the common economic interests that bind them with lower class wage labour.

On the whole, it may be said that, over ten years, a large number of individuals in the higher strata tend to be downgraded resulting into a concentration of ownership over means of production in fewer hands. At the same time the number of individuals in the lower strata tends to become higher and higher with a progressively higher number of individuals in the upper strata loosing control and ownership over the means of production to those who remain in the higher strata. Thus, ownership over means of production tends to be accumulated into ever fewer hands and a large section of the population tends to be downgraded to the lower strata of wage labour.

It is due to the stratum upgradation that agriculturists and farmers among Nadars consider that their occupation is superior to that of parents. Similarly, it is the stratum degradation that is manifested when the farmers and agriculture wage labours among Nairs consider their occupation as inferior to that of their parents. It is the stratum maintenance that makes the wage labour among Nadars and Pulayas consider their position same as their grand parents. The farmers and agriculturists among Nadars are found to be dissatisfied with their present occupation. This is because agriculturists among them want to extend their ownership and control over more land so as to enhance their economic power. Similarly, the farmers among them want to own more land so that they can elevate themselves to the position of agriculturists. It is the process of stratum upgradation that provides this urge for improving their status among the Nair agriculturists and farmers. When the wage labour among Nadars and Pulayas feel satisfied with their occupational position and consequently reconcile with their fate, it is the stratum maintenance that is in

operation. When the agriculturists and farmers want to improve their position by changing their occupation, the wage labour are found to be reconciling to their fate by having no desire to change their occupation.

TABLE 3

Present Occupation Compared to the Occupation of Parents[4]
(Caste-wise)

Castes	*Superior*	*Inferior*	*Same*	*Total*
Nairs	26 (35.14%)	23 (31.08%)	25 (33.78%)	74 (100%)
Nadars	43 (38.05%)	18 (15.93%)	52 (46.02%)	113 (100%)
Pulayas	1 (1.67%)	11 (18.33%)	48 (80%)	60 (100%)
Total	70 (28.35%)	52 (21.05%)	125 (50.60%)	247 (100%)

$X^2_4 = 40.7307$ $X^2_{.99\ (4)} = 13.28$ Significant at 1% level.

TABLE 3A

Present Occupation Compared to the Occupation of Parents[5]
(Class-wise)

Class	*Superior*	*Inferior*	*Same*	*Total*
Upper	36 (75.01%)	7 (14.58%)	5 (10.41%)	48 (100%)
Lower	34 (17.09%)	45 (22.61%)	120 (60.30%)	199 (100%)
Total	70 (28.35%)	52 (21.05%)	125 (50.60%)	247 (100%)

Tenants under absentee landlordism who are engaged in direct cultivation of land may in course of time tend to acquire ownership and control over the land which they cultivate. When this happens, the economic status of such tenants tend to go up and they may acquire upper class status.

Only when members of a caste either acquire control and ownership over more land or loose such ownership and control, there tends to be change in their occupational roles. Instead, if there is no change in the economic status of the members of a group, their occupational status tends to remain the same.

The process by which large number of individuals belonging to the higher strata of the society are brought down to lower strata by means of reducing their control and ownership over means of production and a corresponding downgradation of occupational status may be termed as stratum degradation.

The process by which a large number of individuals from lower strata of a society are elevated to the higher strata by acquiring control and ownership over scarce values of production viz., land and a corresponding acquisition of higher economic status may be termed as stratum upgradation.

The process by which a large section of the population is kept in the lower strata of the society by denying them or withholding from them any control and ownership over the scarce values of production viz., the land and by forcing them to sell their labour for their sustenance may be termed as stratum maintenance.

It may be said that, over the years, a large number of individuals in the higher strata tend to be downgraded resulting into a concentration of ownership over the scarce values of production in fewer hands. At the same time, the number of individuals in the lower strata tends to become higher and higher with a progressively high number of individuals in the upper strata loosing control and ownership over the means of production to those who remain in the higher strata. Thus, ownership over means of production tends to be accumulated into ever fewer hands and a large section of the population tends to be downgraded to the lower strata of the wage labour.

The process of stratum upgradation tends to instill the urge for improving economic status. Stratum maintenance tends to

provide a sense of satisfaction in one's own occupational and economic status.

Attitudes and Values Supporting Economic and Occupational Life

It is the tendency for acquiring more economic power by the higher strata that is revealed, when the Nair and Nadar agriculturists and farmers are found to hold attitudes and values which can foster such a trend. They are found willing to immigrate from the village if they can secure better opportunities. They are also prepared to send their children outside the village for employment. Compared to this, the values held by the wage labour among Nadars, Pulayas and Nairs are found to be for fostering stratum maintenance. There are only very few among them who are prepared to move out of their village. Similarly, it is the process of stratum maintenance that is manifested, when the wage labour among Nairs, Nadars and Pulayas aspire their children also to have same occupation. Compared to this the agriculturists and farmers among Nairs and Nadars want their children to have better status having more earnings.

The persistence of traditional attitudes regarding employment of women is found to be dominant among Nair agriculturists and farmers. Compared to this, agriculturists and farmers among Nadars do not maintain such traditional attitudes. They are found to be in favour of women's employment. As the women among the agricultural wage labour have a tradition for working in the fields even from very early times, there are none among them who disapprove the women's employment. It is probably because of the persistence of traditional values, beliefs and attitudes among the Nairs that facilitated their downgradation in the class hierarchy. It is found that the highest status of the village is assigned to agriculturists followed by farmers.

TABLE 4

Attitudes Towards the Employment of Women[6]

(Caste-wise)

Castes	*Approve*	*Disapprove*	*Total*
Nairs	34 (45.95%)	40 (54.05%)	74 (100%)
Nadars	81 (71.68%)	32 (28 32%)	113 (100%)
Pulayas	48 (80%)	12 (20%)	60 (100%)
Total	163 (66%)	84 (34%)	247 (100%)

$X^2_2 = 13.9138$ $X^2_{.99\ (2)} = 9.21$ Significant at 1% level.

In the case of Nadar agriculturists and farmers, there has been a consistent improvement in their educational attainment over the last three generations. When all their great grand parents were illiterates, a few became literates by the time of grand parents and a substantial section became literates by the time of their parents. At present there are no illiterates among the Nadar agriculturists and farmers. In the case of Nairs it is the reverse trend that is found. When there were no illiterates among them in the earlier generations quite a few have become illiterates by the time of their parents. At present, most of the wage labour and a section of farmers among Nairs are illiterates. As far as the wage labour among Nadars and Pulayas are concerned there has been practically no improvement in their educational attainment. Even now, bulk of them remain as illiterates. But at the same time, it may be noted that, irrespective of caste and class, the villagers aspire to provide better education for their children. This is because,

TABLE 5

Attitudes Towards the Employment of Women[7]
(Class-wise)

Class	Approve				Disapprove				Total
	Nairs	Nadars	Pulayas	Total	Nairs	Nadars	Pulayas	Total	
Upper	14	18	—	32 (62 66%)	15	1	—	16 (33.34%)	48 (100%)
Lower	20	63	48	131 (65.83%)	25	31	12	68 (34.17%)	199 (100%)
Total	34	81	48	163 (66%)	40	32	12	84 (34%)	247 (100%)

with the introduction of compulsory primary education and the phenomenal expansion of higher education, education is considered to be a must for all.

NOTES

1. Appendix I, Q. V-4.
2. *Ibid.*, Q. VI-2.
3. *Ibid*
4. *Ibid.*, Q. VI-3.
5. *Ibid.*
6. *Ibid.*, Q. No. VI-9(*a*).
7. *Ibid.*

CHAPTER TEN

CHANGING PATTERN OF SOCIAL STRATIFICATION

Stratification System

A stratification system may be defined as a pattern or ordering of social relations within a society conforming to an inequitable distribution pattern of scarce values. Stratification system involves hierarchical ordering of economic divisions which are supported by normative and value systems and the patterns of conformity and non-conformity with a corresponding system of rewards and punishments. Based on the degree of control and ownership over the scarce values of social survival, each group is placed on a hierarchy so that those with the maximum degree of control occupy the apex, while the wage labour possessing neither control nor ownership over the scarce values occupy the bottom.

The Inequitable Distribution Pattern of Scarce Values

The values which are necessary for men's survival are scarce. Among them, the means of production constitute the scarcest value and become more and more scarce as time passes and population increases. Closely linked to the scarce values of production are the scarce values of political power which is a social variation of the former. The ownership and control

over these values are distributed among various groups in different measures constituting a differential distribution pattern of scarce values.

Group

A group may be defined as a collectivity of individuals having certain common interests. The members are conscious of this common interest which binds them together.

Upper Class

Those who own land and lives on either the rent from such land or by cultivating such land by employing others without rendering any manual labour by themselves.

Lower Class

The lower class consists of those who are engaged in manual labour either in cultivating their own land or land belonging to others.

The Selected Villages

The Kollal, Vavara and Viakkalloor are the villages which are selected for the study. These three villages from part of the former South Travancore Region, the present Kanyakumari District. The traditional economy in these villages were agricultural and this continues to be the same even now excepting in the distribution pattern of the land ownership which has undergone considerable change. In the early days, Nairs owned the entire land and the agricultural operations used to be carried out with Nadars and Pulayas. But, in later years, particularly after political Independence, Nairs have lost their economic dominance in the villages of Vavara and Kollal and in these two villages the Nadars became economically dominant. In Viakkalloor, there was little change in the economic status of Nairs, Nadars and Pulayas. In the early days, though Nadars and Pulayas constituted the wage labour in the villages, a section among the Nadars emerged as agri-

culturists, by contemporary times, while the remaining Nadars and Pulayas continue to be agricultural labour.

The traditional caste system in this region corresponded with the distribution pattern of the scarce values of land. The Nairs, who owned and controlled the scarce values of land, constituted the upper caste and upper class. The Nadars and Pulayas, who did not have any share in the scarce values of land, remained as lower class and lower caste. When this pattern of the distribution of the scarce values changed with the advent political Independence, traditional caste system also has undergone change. Whenever the lower caste Nadars came to be vested with the ownership and control over the scarce values of land and the Nairs lost their ownership and control, their respective statuses also came to be reversed. The Pulayas, who never had a share in the scarce values of land either in the past or present, remained always as the lower caste and lower class. Thus, in the Kollal village, when the lower caste Nadars became a dominant caste and upper class, the hitherto upper class Nairs came to be relegated to lower class and lower caste status. The Pulayas remained as lower class throughout. In the Vavara village, where the land wealth came to be evenly distributed among Nadars and Nairs, the low caste Nadars had emerged as a dominant caste. As the Pulayas always remained as agricultural labour, there has been very little change in their caste and class status. In the Viakkalloor village, where the Nairs possess the exclusive ownership over the entire scarce values of land, they could always remain as the upper class and upper caste. Both the Nadars and Pulayas in this village have remained as lower castes and the lower class.

Thus, in traditional times, caste used to synchronize with the class in the selected villages. The Nairs who constituted the upper caste were also the upper class. Though there were a number of lower castes among them, only Nadars and Pulayas were numerically dominant.

Till the thirties, Nairs had exclusive ownership over all the cultivable land in the three villages. Consequently, the other

castes were dependant on Nair landlords for their livelihood. In all sectors of socio-economic life, Nairs were in the forefront.

In Kollal and Vavara villages, tenancy system emerged by the time when the Nair joint families were partitioned. The tenants were Nadars and by this time, they could undertake agricultural operations on their own, like the Nairs.

With the conversion to Christianity, social status of Nadars registered further improvement. The conversion to Christianity was more among those Nadars who could improve their economic status. In the Viakkalloor village, where the Nairs could retain their economic dominance, conversion to Christianity was negligible.

When Nairs lost their economic dominance, in Kollal and Vavara villages, they simultaneously lost their political and social dominance. In these villages, the socio-economic and political leadership came to be vested on the newly affluent Nadars.

Thus, when one group looses the economic dominance, they automatically tend to loose their social and political power. The group, which gains economic superiority, tends to gain political as well as social superiorities. When a group retains its economic dominance, it also simultaneously tends to retain social and political dominance as well.

Changing Pattern of Inter-caste Relations

When a group has monopoly over the scarce values of land leaving all other groups economically dependant on them and when such monopoly has been sanctified through religion, beliefs, and value system, then there tends to be very little or no economic competition or rivalry between the economically dominant group and other groups. On the other hand, economic rivalry or competition tends to take place among the members themselves of the group which possesses the monopoly over the scarce values. Those who control or own the larger share of scarce values tend to have maximum support and

following within the group. Also, political power tends to be vested on those having the largest share of scarce values.

So long as a group is numerically dominant and as long as it effectively denied of any control over the scarce values, and if it is reduced to a subordinate status, there tends to emerge greater group solidarity within that group. The group solidarity, which thus emerges, tends to increase so long as such a situation continues. If religion, beliefs and values extend sanctification and legitimisation to such a situation and as long as the dominant group maintains its monopoly over the scarce values, the economically weaker group does not tend to pose any threat to such dominance and the group solidarity within the economically weaker groups tends to be confined to social life alone. When conditions arise for breaking the monopoly of the dominant group over the scarce values, the solidarity among the economically weaker group, which hitherto has been confined to social and cultural spheres alone, tends to extend to the sphere of economic activities. When this happens, the overall solidarity of the economically weaker but the numerically stronger group tends to register a marked increase thereby posing an increasingly greater threat to the monopoly over the scarce values by the economically dominant but the numerically weaker groups. When this happens, all socio-religious sanctifications and legitimisations for the monopoly over the scarce values by the numerically weaker groups tend to disappear and a numerically dominant group tends to acquire more and more control and ownership over the scarce values of production. Once this process begins, there tends to emerge the pauperization of the economically dominant group, which hitherto had the monopoly over the scarce values. Solidarity among the numerically dominant group tends to increase continuously till the group acquires the monopoly over the scarce values. Once the numerically dominant group acquires the monopoly over the scarce values, solidarity tends to decrease leading to the emergence of intra-group rivalries and conflicts. But such intra-group rivalries and conflicts tend to be minimal so long as the solidarity increases.

When a numerically dominant group acquires monopoly

over the scarce values, the group solidarity within that group tends to be minimal giving rise to acute intra-group conflicts and rivalries. But, when such a group looses monopoly over the scarce values and when it tends to become pauperized, group solidarity tends to emerge and intra-group conflicts and rivalries tend to decrease.

When a numerically weaker group does not have any control over the scarce values of production and is kept in subordination for long periods and when such an arrangement is socially sanctified and legitimised, there tends to emerge no solidarity among such groups. Even when the economically dominant group looses monopoly over the scarce values of production, the numerically weaker group, which was in perpetual subordination, does not tend to acquire any share in the scarce values of production.

When a numerically weaker group controls and owns the entire scarce values of production, there tends to emerge a value and belief structure for legitimising and sanctifying such monopoly over the scarce values. When this continues over a long period, the social solidarity within such group tends to decrease and simultaneously intra-group conflicts tend to increase. The rivalries tend to emerge over the possession of scarce values of production and tend to transgress into the spheres of social and political activities. When a numerically weaker section within the same group owns and controls the major portion of the scarce values of production, they tend to become directly involved in the productive activities and as such tend to be more capable for retaining control and ownership over the scarce values. Compared to this the numerically stronger faction tends to be less involved in productive activities and consequently less capable for retaining control and ownership over the scarce values. When these rivalries persist over a long period, conditions may emerge for the group as a whole to loose the control over the scarce values of production. This process tends to be accelerated and the pauperization of the group tends to begin when the institutional sanctifications and legitimisations for the monopoly over the scarce values

disintegrate. When this happens, the group tends to loose, not only the economic power but also the social and political power which it possessed. This loss of economic, political and social power of the numerically weaker group will always tend to benefit the numerically dominant group. But at the same time, the numerically weaker faction within this group tends to sustain only marginal loss of power and, as such, it tends to retain most of the control over the scarce values or production. When the group as a whole sustains the loss of economic, social and political power, it tends to loose its decisive roles in the social, political and economic spheres. The intra-group rivalries and conflicts tend to persist even after the loss of the economic, social and political power till the group as a whole is reduced to a totally subordinate position in the larger society. But when this happens, solidarity tends to emerge and intra-group conflicts and rivalries tend to become minimal. With the emergence of solidarity within the group, those who still retain the control and ownership over the scarce values of production may tend to acquire more and more influence in the social, economic and political life proportional to their share in the scarce values of land.

When a numerically dominant group is denied of any scarce values of production, there tends to emerge a high degree of solidarity within such a group. But united activities and the solidarity as such would tend to be confined to social and cultural life and will not tend to manifest themselves in economic activities as long as institutional sanctifications and legitimisations for their subordination tend to be effective. But as soon as such institutional sanctifications and legitimisations tend to be ineffective, the numerically dominant group tends to develop solidarity among economic activities as well. It also tends to acquire control over more and more scarce values and, in course of time, would replace the numerically weaker group from its dominant positions in socio-economic and political activities. Solidarity tends to go on increasing till near total dominance is established and, once such dominance is established, the solidarity tends to come down. With this decreasing solidarity, intra-group conflicts or rivalries tend to emerge leading to the emergence of factions which would be

headed by richer sections in each faction. In both numerically weaker and numerically stronger groups, the changing pattern of ownership and control over the scarce values of production tends to benefit only a few members of the group concerned and it is these few having ownership and control over the scarce values of production who tend to wield the leadership roles in the groups concerned.

When a numerically weaker group is denied of any control and ownership over the scarce values of production, it always tends to remain as wage labour. When such an arrangement is institutionally sanctified, there tends to emerge more solidarity in such a group. Even after the collapse of legitimisation and sanctification for the subordination of the group, it may still continue in a subordinate position so long as it does not acquire ownership or control over the land. But in the absence of institutional legitimisation for the subordinate position, in course of time, social solidarity may tend to emerge within the group.

When a group possesses monopoly over the scarce values of production and it simultaneously possesses numerical strength, it may continue to retain its monopoly even if institutional legitimisation and sanctification for its monopoly disappears. So long as the members of the group are directly involved in productive activities, they do not tend to loose control and ownership over the scarce values. Social solidarity tends to be minimal, so long as there are institutional legitimisation and sanctification for the monopoly over the scarce values. But once such institutional sanctification and legitimisation disappear and similar group in the larger society loses its monopoly over the scarce values of land, social solidarity within the group tends to emerge and intra-group rivalries and conflict tend to become minimal. Social interaction tends to increase and the group as a whole tends to emerge as an organized one. The leadership of the group tends to be vested on those having the largest share in the scarce values of production. When a group which possesses only an equal numerical strength as the group having the monopoly over the scarce value of production, it does not tend to acquire more share in the scarce values. Social

solidarity in such a group tends to be high in social and cultural spheres while solidarity in economic sphere may be minimal so long as institutional sanctifications and legitimisations for the subordinate position exist. Once such institutional arrangements collapse, solidarity in economic sphere also emerges and, when this happens, the group may come into conflict with that group which wields monopoly over the scarce values. But such conflicts do not tend to enhance the economic status of the group and, on the contrary, they may tend to affect the economic interests of the group adversely. When a numerically dominant group is totally denied of any share in the scarce values of production and the institutional sanctifications and legitimisations for such denial exist over long periods, there tends to be no solidarity within such a group. Even if the institutional arrangements for subordination disappear, solidarity in such groups does not tend to emerge, so long as there is total economic dependance on the economically dominant group.

Caste Stratification and Economic Conflict

Group solidarity tends to be less within the upper caste which simultaneously constitutes the upper class. Group solidarity tends to be high within the lower caste which has only partial dependance on the upper caste. When the lower caste constitutes the lower class and when there is total economic dependance on the upper caste, group solidarity tends to be less within such lower caste.

When the upper caste constitutes the upper class, there tends to be increasing economic rivalry within the upper caste. This economic conflict within the upper caste tends to deprive it of its upper class position. The lower caste, which is only partially dependant on the upper caste in economic pursuits, tends to improve its economic status. In course of time the upper caste tends to be reduced to the lower class position and the lower caste tends to be raised to upper class position.

When a lower caste is totally dependant on upper caste which is also the upper class in the economic sphere, there

tends to be of no improvement in the economic status of the lower class but their economic dependance may shift from the upper caste to those lower castes which may become the new upper class.

In the economic transactions between the upper caste and the partially dependant lower caste, the latter always tends to benefit through such transactions. In course of time, the upper caste may tend to be reluctant to enter into economic transactions with the partially dependant lower caste while the latter tends to take initiative in such transactions. In the case of totally dependant lower caste, there tends to be no inhibition on economic transaction between them and those castes who occupy the upper class position.

In such a situation the upper caste tends to be reduced to lower class position and, in course of time, may be considered as a lower caste. The lower caste, which is only partially dependant on upper caste, tends to occupy the upper class position and, in course of time, may tend to assume upper class status. Those lower castes, who are totally dependant on upper castes, tend to stagnate in their lower class positions. They tend to remain always as the lower castes.

Caste Stratification and Political Activities

When traditional caste hierarchy synchronizes with the differential distribution pattern of the scarce values of land, political power tends to be vested on the caste which is at the apex of the caste hierarchy and having economic power. When the traditional caste hierarchy undergoes change and a caste lower in the hierarchy rises to the apex, and when it acquires economic power, the political power also tends to be vested on the lower caste which has thus risen to the apex in the caste hierarchy. When caste stratification transforms itself into caste association, economic power no more tends to be an exclusive preserve of a particular caste. On the other hand economic power tends to be shared between the castes who are numerically dominant and nearer to each other at the apex of the caste hierarchy. When this happens the numerically dominant

caste, with the introduction of adult franchise, will tend to rise to the apex of the caste hierarchy thereby relegating the hitherto highest castes to secondary positions.

Political power tends to gravitate towards economic power. The emergent upper caste which replaces the traditional upper caste tends to assume political power positions. When this happens, a section among the traditional upper caste tends to be reduced to the status of wage labour. Also wage labour among different castes tend to come closer together in economic relations. There tends to be rivalry between the affluent section among the dominant castes for securing power positions in political activities. These rivalries tend to assume caste-wise cleavages. The affluent section in the dominant caste which possesses the maximum share of economic power tends to assume the political leadership. In political activities, the next dominant caste in the emergent hierarchy tends to secure only secondary positions of leadership, and this tends to be vested only on the affluent section within that caste. Only those among the wage labour in various caste groups who are economically dependant on affluent sections alone tend to extend their support to the ruling political party. A section of the wage labour in all castes tend to support the non-ruling opposition party. When the traditional caste hierarchy synchronizes with the distribution pattern of the scarce values of land and does not undergo any change, the upper caste always tends to extend their support to the ruling political party. In other words, when the ruling political party looses its power and it is replaced by another, the upper caste would tend to shift their allegiance to the emergent ruling party.

Caste Stratification and Social and Educational Activities

Improvement in the economic status tends to improvement in the educational status. With any deterioration in the economic status, there tends to be a corresponding deterioration in the educational status also. When there is no appreciable change in the economic status, there tends to be a little change in the educational status. When there is competition between

two groups in economic activities, there tends to emerge competition between them in the field of education and socio-cultural activities. In such competitions, or conflicts, the dominant group tends to be the one which possesses and holds the dominant share of scarce values of land. When caste stratification synchronizes with the class stratification, the caste stratification tends to extend to the spheres of socio-cultural and educational activities. But as soon as caste stratification ceases to synchronize with class stratification, it will be the class stratification that tends to prevail in the fields of socio-cultural and educational activities. When members of the dominant caste loose control over the scarce values of land to the members of the lower caste, the traditional caste hierarchy tends to become irrelevant leading to the emergence of caste associations which do not fit into the traditional hierarchy. In such situation, the lower caste as a whole may become the dominant caste in the field of education and socio-political activities, if the members of that caste come to own and control the bulk of the scarce values of land in the area. When this happens in the immediate larger society, the new socio-cultural and educational opportunities acquired by the lower caste come to be enjoyed by the same lower caste in a smaller community where there may not be any improvement in their economic status. But such phenomena are to be explained in terms of the larger change that is taking place in the caste and class stratifications in the larger society.

Changing Pattern of Intra-caste Relations

In a stratification system, where social interaction between the strata are minimal while there is total economic dependance by the entire lower strata on those of the upper caste at the apex, there tends to be an inhibition of awareness among the lower strata about the common interests and common social characteristics that can bind them. Under such a system, there tends to be no conflict in relation between the upper strata and the lower strata. Intra-strata conflicts tend to arise when conflicting relations between strata are inhibited. When the stratification is caste stratification, the intra-strata conflicts tend to be intra-caste conflicts. Under such a caste stratification

system, solidarity within each caste tends to be minimal. Any threat to the economic dominance of upper caste (strata) tends to be from within the same caste. Intra-caste conflicts among upper caste or upper strata tends to be primarily in the field of economic activities. But such intra-caste conflicts may tend to transgress into social and political fields. It is the conflicts among the upper class sections which always tend to assume the form of inter-caste conflicts. Caste affiliations tend to protect the economic interests of only the upper class sections in each caste. Though the lower class section in each caste may believe that caste affiliations serve to safeguard their economic interests, in reality, they do not tend to derive any economic benefit through caste affiliations. On the other hand they tend to be exploited by making them accept low wages in the name of caste solidarity. The horizontal caste groupings tend to help the upper class sections in each caste, by enabling them to extend their dominance in the economic field to the educational and political fields. The social life of the lower class section in each caste tends to be confined to their own caste permitting little interaction between the castes. In the case of upper class section of each caste, social interaction tends to cut across caste affiliations. Their economic dominance tends to transgress not only to the political field but also to the field of education. In this, caste groupings tend to facilitate the upper classes and the middle classes to derive educational benefits while denying the same to the lower classes. As in the traditional caste stratification, higher education tends to be the exclusive preserve of upper and middle classes.

Caste solidarity in the lower caste consisting of wage labour may tend to contribute to their bargaining capacity for better wages and working conditions. It may also tend to promote greater social interaction within the group and may tend to inhibit factionalism. The total economic dependance of such groups may tend to prevent the members from making any substantial benefits in social, political and educational fields. Inter-caste conflicts tend to be primarily around the conflicting economic interests of the upper classes among different castes. But such conflicts tend to assume non-economic character when

wage labour in the conflicting castes are also brought into the dispute on the basis of caste affiliations. Though inter-caste conflicts benefit only the upper classes, the lower class participants tend to be active even though they do not derive any benefit from such disputes. In other words, caste membership and caste consciousness function for safeguarding the economic interests of the upper classes and at the same time they tend to facilitate the economic exploitation of the lower classes.

Caste cleavages tend to extend to the political field. It is always the upper class section among each caste which tends to derive political benefits from the extension of caste cleavages to the political field. Caste groups which consist exclusively of agricultural labourers tend to divide their political allegiance between the upper class sections in other castes.

Caste solidarity tends to inhibit intra-caste conflicts. As most of the inter-caste conflicts are confined to economic field, the beneficiaries of inhibitions on intra-caste conflicts tend to be the upper class section in the castes which are involved in such conflicts.

When a group which has only minimal control over the scarce values of land and when most of its members are wage labours, such a group tends to be always adversely affected in the economic and political fields when it comes into conflict with the dominant group which possesses control and ownership over most of the scarce values of land. When this happens, the worst sufferers tend to be the wage labour in the weaker group. If there is a third group which consists exclusively of wage labour and is economically dependant on the dominant group, then it would be the wage labour in this group that tends to derive economic benefits from the disputes between the dominant groups. In such a situation, caste solidarity tends to create cleavages on the basis of caste among the wage labour themselves, thereby radically affecting the economic interests of the wage labour as a whole. At the same time upper class section in the dominant group always tends to derive economic benefits. Also, this section tends to derive political and educational benefits as well.

When hierarchical caste stratification is subsuituted by class stratification and horizontal caste groupings, caste affiliation and caste solidarity tend to persist and they tend to reinforce the dominant position of the upper class in the economic and political fields. Caste tends to be the basis for kinship relations like marriage even though such kinship relations tend to be confined to each class within the caste groupings. As far as the lower class sections in different castes are concerned, social interaction tends to be confined to the respective lower class section within each caste. But in the case of upper class in various castes, social interaction may tend to cut across caste boundaries.

Caste Stereotypes

Competitive and conflicting relations may tend to the emergence of caste stereotypes. Each caste tends to attribute all unfavourable and undesirable characteristics on those castes which are opposed to it. Similarly, all favourable and desirable characteristics tend to be attributed to those who belong to one's own caste. When a caste develops caste solidarity, it may develop caste stereotypes regarding other castes, especially, those castes which are economically or socially superior.

The emergence of caste association tends to inhibit the emergence of class consciousness among the weaker section in different castes. Caste relations tend to safeguard the economic, political and educational interests of the upper class sections in different castes. Even though caste associations do not safeguard the interests of lower classes, they tend to strengthen their respective caste associations when they develop caste identification with the upper class section in their respective caste group.

Economy and Traditional Value System

When caste stratification synchronizes with class stratification, social interaction tends to be confined to each caste. Intra-caste interactions tend to be minimal. The belief and

value systems tend to preserve caste insultations by restricting inter-caste interactions. The belief and value systems tend to reinforce social distance practices by providing ideological justifications for the social separation between castes.

When caste stratification is replaced by horizontal caste groupings, the belief and value systems which used to support social distance practices may tend to be replaced by new belief and value systems which would no more restrict inter-caste social interactions. When this happens, inter-caste social interactions tend to increase.

Religious Faith and Changing Value System

When the distribution pattern of the scarce value of production undergoes change resulting into a re-organization of the traditional stratification systems, beliefs, and values which hitherto, have been supporting traditional stratification also tend to undergo change. Among those sections of people whose economic status undergoes change, there tends to be decline in the faith in supernatural power. At the same time faith in supernatural power tends to persist among those sections of people whose economic status remains static. Thus, it may be said that any change in the distribution pattern of scarce values tends to bring about corresponding changes in the belief and value system.

Religious beliefs and values tend to reinforce the differential distribution pattern of scarce values by inhibiting intra-structural change in the society. Subordination and subjection of wage labour tend to be perpetuated by belief in re-birth and fate. Simultaneously such beliefs also tend to inhibit any challenge or threat to the differential distribution pattern of scarce values from those who do not possess any control or ownership over the scarce values of production. The traditional values and beliefs tend to loose their efficacy and influence when the traditional hierarchical caste system looses its economic foundation. The declining belief in supernatural power and the growing recognition of man's own capacity to change socio-economic condition as against leaving them to the hands of

supernatural power tend to be the manifestation of economic changes which in turn lead to the change in the stratification system. The declining faith in supernatural power and the declining influence of beliefs in fate and re-birth tend to be confined to those sections or castes who possess either control or ownership over the scarce values of production. The traditional values and beliefs tend to persist only among wage labours who do not possess any control or ownership over the scarce values of production. The persistence of belief in supernatural power, fate and re-birth among the wage labour tend to inhibit their initiative for improving their socio-economic condition. It is this process which tends to ensure a sustained supply of cheap labour for agricultural operations. The observance of religious ceremonies tends to decline among the upper classes while at the same time it tends to persist among the lower classes.

Class Categories

Under the traditional caste stratification, the upper classes constituted the upper castes and the lower classes constituted the lower castes. The upper castes possessed exclusive control and ownership over the scarce values of land. The lower castes used to be the wage labour and as such they were economically dependant on the upper castes.

When a few among the lower classes who constituted the lower castes acquire ownership over the scarce values of land, they tend to acquire upper class status. When this happens, the traditional caste stratification ceases to synchronize with class stratification. With this the traditional caste system tends to disintegrate. In a lower caste if there is no one who could acquire control or ownership over the scarce values of land, there tends to be no change in the class status of such caste.

Class stratification tends to be essentially dichotomous with two classes of upper and lower depending on whether those included in two classes are engaged in manual labour or not. But people tend to visualize a trichotamic class division of

upper, lower, and middle. All those who are engaged in manual labour tend to be included under the lower class. The distinction between the upper class and the middle class is more superficial than real. This is because the basis of this distinction is only the differential income of the people concerned.

In the traditional society, when the lower class used to be constituted exclusively by the lower castes, by contemporary times, the lower class is composed of all those who are engaged in manual labour and as such they belong to both upper and lower castes. This indicates that, with the changing distribution pattern of the scarce values, there tends to be corresponding changes in the system of stratification.

In contemporary society, wealth and income tend to be the exclusive factors in determining class position. At the same time caste tends to be no more considered as a determinant factor behind class position. Consequently, for holding upper class status, upper caste membership tends to be no more an important criteria. The upper class position tends to be determined only by high income and wealth. It is because of this that those among the lower castes who have acquired wealth and high income tend to acquire upper class status. Similarly those among the upper castes who had lost control and ownership over their land and thus became the wage labour tend to be reduced to the status of lower class. But within the emergent upper class, status differentiation tends to be on the basis of certain non-economic factors such as family status and political power.

Changing Pattern of Class Stratification

In the traditional society, those who owned and controlled the scarce values of land constituted not only the upper class but also upper castes. In other words, the traditional caste system enabled the upper classes to perpetuate their upper class position. When a numerically weaker upper caste possesses exclusive control and ownership over the scarce values of land and a numerically dominant lower caste is denied of any share in the control and ownership over the scarce values of land and

the upper caste can exploit the land wealth only with the help of the immediately lower but the numerically dominant lower caste, there tends to emerge a section among such lower caste who would try to acquire control or ownership over the land. Consequently, this section among the lower caste may succeed in acquiring control or ownership over land. This redistribution of scarce values of land among both the upper caste and a section of lower caste may bring about pauperization of a section of the upper caste. Simultaneously, that section of the lower castes who acquires ownership and control over the land may assume upper class status. When this happens a new class stratification may arise which would replace the traditional one. This transformation of class stratification may take place through generations.

Those lower castes, which are numerically smaller, may not acquire any control over the scarce values of land. If this happens they tend to remain as lower class even under the emergent class stratification.

Intra-class Relations

When class stratification no more synchronizes with caste stratification, intra-class relations tend to prevail over inter-caste relations. Similarly inter-class relations tend to prevail over intra-caste relations. Class orientation tends to replace caste orientation in social, educational and political interaction. In political activities interaction tends to be more class-based.

When upper caste persons having upper class background are reduced to lower class status, they tend to retain their upper class orientation and values. Lower class persons may tend to identify themselves with upper class when they are anxious to improve their socio-economic status.

When caste and class cease to synchronize, class background tends to be the basis for neighbourhood relations, personal relations, and political relations, caste tends to continue to the basis for kinship relations. But if caste background is the same, class tends to be the basis for kinship relations also.

Inter-class Relations

Inter-class relations tend to be the same as inter-caste relations when class stratification superimposes over caste stratification. Under such conditions, the upper class who, simultaneously constitutes the upper castes, tend to have minimal interaction with the lower class who also constitutes the lower castes in social, political and cultural fields. When inter-caste mobility is strictly forbidden, there tends to be no inter-class mobility. Social distance practices under the caste system tend to reinforce the class based super-ordinate-subordinate inter-class relations. The religious approval and sanctification behind the class based caste system tend to foster harmonious inter-class relations and, at the same time, they simultaneously tend to inhibit strained and conflicting relations between the classes.

When caste ceases to synchronize with class, inter-caste relations tend to be conflicting and strained. Similarly inter-class relations also tend to be strained. The super-ordinate-subordinate relations that hitherto characterized the inter-caste relations cease to synchronize with upper caste-lower caste relationship. In other words, super-ordinate-subordinate relations will be the basis for inter-class relations and not inter-caste relationship.

Even when caste stratification no more synchronizes with class stratification, among the lower classes, caste affiliation tends to continue as the basis for interactions in social life. But among the upper classes, social interaction tends to be on the basis of class affiliation rather than caste affiliation. Thus, it can be said that social interaction tends to assume more and more class characteristics while shedding the caste characteristics when class ceases to super-impose over caste. The social distance practices which used to characterise the interaction in traditional society tend to persist in the case of inter-class relations while at the same time they tend to be minimal in the case of inter-caste relations.

When caste stratification ceases to superimpose over class stratification, class based stereo-types tend to emerge characterizing the conflicting relations between the classes.

Caste and Class Stratification and Leadership

Under the traditional caste stratification where caste synchronizes with class, political leadership tends to be vested on the numerically smaller upper castes. Any threat to the economic interest of the upper caste from the numerically larger lower castes tends to be curbed by using the political authority vested on the upper castes. When the traditional caste stratification undergoes change through the induction of a section of the lower castes to the upper class, political authority ceases to be the exclusive preserve of the upper castes and instead, it tends to be shared by all upper class sections belonging to the different caste groups. When this happens, political leadership tends to be determined by class status and numerical support. Also caste ceased to be the major determining factor behind leadership. Thus, it can be said that, when caste stratification ceases to synchronize with class stratification, political leadership tends to be determined by class status rather than caste status.

Class Status and Leadership

When persons, from lower castes acquire ownership and control over a substantial part of cultivable land wealth, they can replace the traditional political leadership by taking political leadership in their own hand. Their identification with their own caste which is numerically stronger but lower in the traditional caste hierachy tends to enable them to secure greater numerical support in the community as a whole. This also tends to increase their political authority. When this happens, the upper castes which wielded political power under the traditional caste system, tend to loose their political power simultaneously when they loose their control and ownership over their land. In other words, political power always tends to be vested on the upper class section irrespective of their caste and sectarian background. When a lower caste consists exclusively of agricultural wage labour, it tends to be always excluded

from political authority. Political authority tends to be denied to all lower class sections irrespective of their caste background. The numerical strength of a caste tends to be decisive in determining political leadership only when a section among them either own or control the scarce values of production. Even if a caste group is numerically dominant, it may not get any share in the political power if it does not control or own the scarce values of production. In other words, numerical strength by itself does not determine political power. It tends to function only as a contributory factor to class status, is determining political leadership.

Determinants of Leadership

Irrespective of the nature of stratification system prevalent, it is always those who own and control the scarce values of production who tend to be vested with political leadership. In other words, political leadership tends to be vested on upper class section. Under the traditional system of caste stratification, as caste and class were complementary, both tended to determine political leadership. Even when caste ceases to synchronize with class in the emergent system of stratification, caste tends to persist in exercising influence in leadership. But the role of caste in determining leadership, when caste and class do not synchronize with class. When caste and class do not synchronize, the role of caste tends to be for reinforcing the influence of upper class section over the lower class section. When there were no upper classes within a particular caste and members of the caste are mostly agricultural wage labour, it is the economic dependance of such caste on the upper class section in other castes which would tend to determine their political behaviour. The lower class section in each caste tends to extend their political support to the upper class section in the same caste. In other words, it can be said that when class background being the same, it is the sectarian background that tends to determine political leadership.

The influence and power which the leaders possess tend to be derived from the upper class status rather than their

caste status. Caste background is only supplementary to class status.

The upper class section tend to shift their political party affiliation so that they may always constitute the ruling group. It is the economic interests rather than the ideological interests that tend to be the motivating force behind the shifting political allegiance. It is because of this fact that the political support for the ruling parties tends to be derived mostly from the upper class section. Similarly political support for non-ruling political parties tends to be derived from the lower class section. But even here, leadership of such non-ruling political parties tends to be vested on the upper class section.

It is the economic self-interests that tend to determine the political allegiance of upper classes. At the same time, it is the ideological considerations that tend to determine the political allegiance of lower classes. But here the ideological considerations may be indirectly economic interests in the sense that the lower classes tend to extend their support to non-ruling political parties under the impression that such parties may strive to improve their economic conditions. But whatever may be the ideological orientations of the party that comes into power, the upper class always tends to join the ruling party for making use of the political power to safeguard their economic interests.

Traditional Caste and Class Stratification, Occupation and Economic Life

So long as the basic economy of the society continues to be agricultural, the occupational pattern may tend to persist. If the class stratification synchronizes with caste stratification as in traditional Indian society, the occupational pattern tends to conform with the caste stratification. The moment class stratification ceases to superimpose over caste stratification, occupational pattern may also cease to synchronize with caste stratification and instead, it may tend to conform only with class stratification.

Changing Pattern of Occupational Life

Any redistribution of land ownership in agricultural economy tends to bring about a corresponding redistribution of occupational roles in different castes. But such a redistribution of occupational roles tends to be confined to only those sections of the caste who come to acquire either ownership or control over the scarce values of land.

When those, who own the scarce values of land, do not directly cultivate and instead live on the rent from such land, they may tend to loose their ownership over the land. When this happens, such sections may tend to be reduced to lower class status. In other words, absentee landlordism, if persists over long periods, may tend to bring about the pauperization of landlords. When owners of the land are engaged in direct cultivation, they tend to remain their upper class status. In short, it may be said that if upper classes in agricultural economy live on land rent, their economic dominance tends to decline in course of time. On the other hand, if the upper classes effectively control the productive activities through direct participation, their economic status either tends to go up or tends to be retained as such.

Stratum Degradation and Stratum Upgradation

Under absentee landlordism, those tenants, who are engaged in direct cultivation of land, main course of time tends to acquire ownership and control over their land which they cultivate. When this happens, the economic status of such tenants tend to go up and they may acquire upper class status.

Only when members of the caste either acquire control and ownership over more land or loose such ownership and control, there tend to be change in their occupational status. If there is no change in the economic status of the members of a group, their occupational status tends to remain the same.

The process by which large number of individuals belonging to the higher strata are brought down to the lower strata by

means of reducing their control and ownership over means of production and a corresponding downgradation of occupational status may be termed as stratum degradation.

The process by which a large number of individuals from the lower strata of the society are elevated to the upper strata by acquiring control and ownership over scarce values of production viz., land and a corresponding acquisition of higher economic status may be termed as stratum upgradation.

The process by which a large section of the population is kept in the lower strata of the society by denying them or with-holding from them any control and ownership over scarce values of production viz., the land and by forcing them to sell their labour for their sustenance may be termed as stratum maintenance.

Over the years, a large number of individuals in the higher strata tend to be downgraded resulting into a concentration of ownership over the scarce values of production in fewer hands. At the same time, the number of individuals in the lower strata tends to become higher and higher with a progressively number of individuals in the upper strata loosing their control and ownership over means of production to those who remain in the higher strata. Thus ownership over means of production tends to be accumulated in ever fewer hands and a large section of the population tend to be downgraded to the lower strata of the wage labour.

The process of stratum upgradation tends to instill the urge for improving economic status. Stratum maintenance tends to provide a sense of satisfaction in one's own occupational and economic status.

Attitudes and Values Supporting Economic and Occupational Life

It can be said that the attitudes and values which are held by members belonging to each strata tend to foster their

economic and political status. The processes of stratum upgradation and stratum maintenance tend to be reinforced by attitudes and values which emerge out of such processes. When traditional beliefs, values and attitudes which do not support stratum upgradation are held by a section of the upper strata, such sections tend to be downgraded in the class hierarchy.

Educational status tends to be directly related to economic status. Those who acquire higher status tend to acquire simultaneously higher educational status also. The educational status tends to be low and stagnant when there is no improvement in the economic status.

APPENDIX I

Changing Pattern of Social Stratification in Kerala

Miss Thara Bhai
Ph. D. Research Scholar
Department of Sociology
University of Kerala.

INTERVIEW SCHEDULE

(Information collected will be kept strictly confidential and will be used only for academic inquiry)

I. Background Data

(*a*) *Personal Data* :

(1) Name (2) Sex
(3) Age (4) Religion
(5) Caste (6) Education (Primary/Secondary/College/Professional)
(7) Occupation (8) Monthly income

(*b*) *Family Data :*

No.	Name	Relation to the informant	Age	Marital status (Single/married/widowed/separated)	Education (Primary/Secondary College/Professional)	Occupation

II. Data on Class Stratification

1. Please indicate the class categories found in your village and the income groups to which they fall.

Class category	Income group
(*i*) Upper Class	
(*ii*) Upper Middle Class	
(*iii*) Middle Class	
(*iv*) Lower Middle Class	
(*v*) Lower Class	

2 Kindly specify the class category among the following to which you belong.

(*i*) Upper Class (*ii*) Upper Middle Class
(*iii*) Middle Class (*iv*) Lower Middle Class
(*v*) Lower Class

3. To which class category you will place your parents, grand-parents and great grand parents.

(*i*) Parents Upper Class/Upper Middle Class/Middle Class/Lower Middle Class/Lower Class.

(*ii*) Grand parents Upper Class/Upper Middle Class/Middle Class/Lower Middle Class/Lower Class.

(*iii*) Great grand parents Upper Class/Upper Middle Class/Middle Class/Lower Middle Class/Lower Class.

4. If they do not belong to the same class category as you belong, can you give the reasons for the same ?

Parents
Grand parents
Great grand parents

5. Please give the names of three individuals from each class categories found in your village and also the caste background of each person.

Class	Name	Caste	Name	Caste	Name	Caste

6. According to you what are the important characteristics which determines upper class positions in your village ? Specify items in the order of importance.

1. Income 2. Caste 3. Political power 4. Religious belief 5. Family background 6. Others (Specify if any)

7. What kind of relationship you have with the members of classes below yours ?
   Equal/Superior (look down on them)

8. What kind of relationship you have with members of class above yours ?
   Equal/Inferior (look upon them)

9. (*a*) Do you keep any social distance with the members of other classes ?
   Yes/No
   (*b*) How ?

10. Do you think that upper class people always try to maintain their class positions ?
    Yes/No

11. Do you think that it is possible for lower class people to improve their status positions by getting into upper class positions ?
    Yes/No

12. If yes, can you give some reasons for it ?
    (*i*) (*ii*) (*iii*) (*iv*)

13. Whom do you prefer the following :
    (*i*) For marital Relationship
    Upper/Upper Middle/Middle/Lower Middle/Lower

    (*ii* Is Panchayat President
    Upper/Upper Middle/Middle/Lower Middle/Lower

    (*iii*) To represent your constituency
    Upper/Upper Middle/Middle/Lower Middle/Lower

    (*iv*) As a personal friend
    Upper/Upper Middle/Middle/Lower Middle/Lower

    (*v*) As a neighbour
    Upper/Upper Middle/Middle/Lower Middle/Lower

14. What is your concept or image of the upper classes or rich in your village ?
    Vicious, Unscrupulous, God-fearing, Religious minded, helping, Philanthropic, Stingy, specify any other.

15. What is your concept or image of the lower class or poor in your village ?
    Contemptible, unscrupulous, vicious, God-fearing, Religious minded, helping, philanthropic, specify any other.

III. Caste

1. (*a*) What do you think of the caste solidarity which exists today in your village as compared to what was prevalent before independence ?

    Same as before/increased/decreased.

    (*b*) Give reasons.
    (*i*) (*ii*) (*iii*) (*iv*)

2. Does your caste membership facilitate your activities in any of the following fields.
    i. Economic Yes/No *ii.* Social Yes/No
    iii. Political Yes/No *iv.* Educational Yes/No

3. (*a*) Do you depend on caste for any thing ? Yes/No
   (*b*) If Yes, what are they ?
   (*i*) (*ii*) (*iii*) (*iv*)

4. In what way each caste in your village has been affected after Independence in the following fields ?

Field activities	Nairs	Nadars	Pulayas
Economic	Improved/deteriorated/ no change	Improved/ deteriora-ted/no change	Improved/ deteriora-ted/no change
Political	Improved/deteriorated/ no change	Improved/ deteriora-ted/no change	Improved/ deteriora-ted/no change
Social	Improved/deteriorated/ no change	Improved/ deteriora-ted/ no change	Improved/ deteriora-ted/no change
Education	Improved/deteriorated/ no change	Improved/ deteriora-ted/no change	Improved/ deteriora-ted/no change.

5. According to you what is the nature of relation which your caste has with other castes in the village in the following fields.

   (*i*) With Nairs/Nadars/Pulayas

   (*a*) Economic — Competitive or conflict/cordial/ indifferent
   (*b*) Educational — Competitive or conflict/cordial/ indifferent

(c) Political — Competitive or conflict/cordial/indifferent

(d) Social — Competitive or conflict/cordial/indifferent.

(ii) With Nairs/Nadars/Pulayas

(a) Economic — Competitive or conflict/cordial/indifferent

(b) Educational — Competitive or conflict/cordial/indifferent

(c) Political — Competitive or conflict/cordial/indifferent

(d) Social — Competitive or conflict/cordial/indifferent.

6. Do you think that the nature of relation with other castes change with the changing interests or goals which your castes or other castes have in each field.

Yes/No

7. Whom do you prefer for the following :

(i) For marital relationship
(Nairs/Nadars/Pulayas/No caste preference)

(ii) As a personal friend
(Nairs/Nadars/Pulayas/No caste preference)

(iii) As a neighbour
(Nairs/Nadars/Pulayas/No caste preference)

(iv) As a Panchayat president
(Nairs/Nadars/Pulayas No caste preference)

(v) To represent your legislative constituency
(Nairs/Nadars/Pulayas/No caste preference)

(vi) For economic transactions
(Nairs/Nadars/Pulayas/No caste preference)

8. Please specify the most influential leaders of your village in the following fields.

	Name	Caste	Class	Name	Caste	Class	Name	Caste	Class
(*i*) Economic									
(*ii*) Political									
(*iii*) Educational									
(*iv*) Social									

9. Give the names of two closest personal or family friends.

Name *Caste* *Class*

10. For various functions like marriage in your family whom do you invite among the following castes ?

Nairs/Nadars/Pulayas

11. Do you observe any social distance like pollution with reference to any of the following castes in your village ?
    1. Nairs None/Specify if observed
    2. Nadars None/Specify if observed
    3. Pulayas None/Specify if observed

12. Do you help your caste members when need arises in any of the following fields ?

(*i* Economic Yes/No (*ii*) Political Yes/No
(*iii*) Educational Yes/No *iv*' Social Yes/No

13. Do you stand for your caste whenever critical situations arises vis-a-vis its relation with other castes ?

Yes/No

14. According to you who are the three most influential leaders of your caste in the village ?

Sl. No. *Name* *Class*

15. According to you what are the essential prerequisites for a

person to become a caste leader ? Name them according to priority ?

(1) High income or wealth (2) Strong religious belief
(3) Family background (4) Political influence
(5) Prestigious Occupation (6) Specify any other

16. Do you think that caste considerations determine the nature of voting during elections ?

Yes/No

17. Do you take into account your caste interests in exercising in your franchise (Vote) ?

Yes/No

18. Do you think that caste system is necessary even today ?

Yes/No

Give reasons for your opinion.

19. Are you in favour of a casteless society ?

Yes/No

20. What is your concept or image of the following :

(*i*) Nairs Crooked, unscrupulous, straightforward, stingy, large-hearted, religious minded, communal.

(*ii*) Nadars Crooked, unscrupulous, straightforward, stingy, large-hearted, religious minded, communal.

(*iii*) Pulayas Crooked, unscrupulous, straightforward, stingy, large-hearted, religious minded, communal.

IV. Data on the Pattern of Power Distribution and Leadership

1. In every village there will be some influential person who are having more power than others. Do you agree with this statement as far as your village is concerned ?

Yes/No

2. If the answer is negative give reasons.

3. Please name three influential persons for your village in the order of their importance.

   Name *Caste* *Class*

4. According to you what is the basis of their power ? Mark the most important ones in the order of the importance.

   (1) Financial position (2) Physical Force
   (3) Caste leader (4) Family reputation
   (5) Influence in social and political fields (6) Philanthropy
   (7) Occupational status (8) If any other specify

5. To whom did you give your votes in the last Panchayat election ?
   People having power/Caste people/according to political party/upper class or rich/Lower class or poor/any other.

6. To which political party you belong or support during elections ?
   D.M.K /C.P.M./C.P.I./R.S.P./Muslim League/Congress (O)/ Congress (N)/Swatantra/Any other (Specify)

7. What made you join or support it ?
   Caste considerations/Class considerations/Ideological/any other.

8. Which political party your father and great grand father supported ?
   (*i*) Father
   (*ii*) Great grand father

9. In the past election have you given your vote to the same party as the one supported by your parents or grand parents ?

   Yes/No

10. If you have changed your party since the last elections, please give the reasons.

11. What are the important considerations which influence the elections in your village ?

    1. Economic 2. Caste
    3. Political Party 4. If any other specify

V. Economic Background

1. Is the house in which you live your own or rented ?
   own/rented

2. If it is your own how did you get it ?
   Acquired/Inherited

3. How much landed properties your own ?

   Acres *Cents* *Current money value*

4. How much landed properties your parents, grand parents and great grand parents had ?

	Acres	*Cents*	*Current money value*
Parents			
Grand Parents			
Great Grand Parents			

5. How much property you brought by your own effort and how much you inherited ?

	Acres	*Cents*	*Money values*
Acquired			
Inherited			

6. Can you name three landlords of your village according to priority ?

	Caste	*Class*
1.		
2.		
3.		

VI. Occupational Background

1. What was your father's, grand father's and great grand father's occupation ?

   (*i*) Father
   (*ii*) Grand father
   (*iii*) Great grand father

2. Is your occupation hereditary ?
   Yes/No

3. Compared to the occupations of your parents, what do you think of your occupation ?
   Superior/Inferior/Same

4. Do you feel satisfied with your present occupation ?
   Yes/No

5. (*a*) Do you think of changing your present occupation ?
   Yes/No
   (*b*) If Yes, give reasons.

6. Will you go outside the village for the sake of employment ?
   Yes/No

7. Will you let your children to go outside the village for employment ?
   Yes/No

8. What occupation you are aspiring for your son ?
Same occupation/a job which earns more/according to his preference ?

9. (*a*) What is your opinion regarding women going for employment ?
Approve/Disapprove
(*b*) Please give the reasons for your view.

10. Please name the occupations, which you consider as having high status in your village.
(1) (2) (3)

VII. Educational Background

1. Please give the details of educational attainment of your following relatives.
(*i*) Father (*ii*) Grand father (*iii*) Great grand father
(*iv*) Mother (*v*) Grand mother (*vi*) Great grand mother

2. How much education you aspire for your children ?
(*i*) Daughters (*ii*) Sons

3. Do you consider education is a 'must' today ?
Yes/No

VIII. Religion and Moral Code

1. Do you use alcoholic beverages ?
Yes/No

2. Do you consider the following as bad habits ?
(*a*) Smoking Yes/No
(*b*) Drinking Yes/No

3. Does your children, you and your parents attend temple/church/mosques ?
(*i*) Children Regularly/Occasionally/Never
(*ii*) You Regularly/Occasionally/Never
(*iii*) Parents Regularly/Occasionally/Never

4. Do you observe religious ceremonies ?

Regularly/Occasionally/Never

IX. Social Distance among Nadars, Pulayas and Nairs

1. Do you invite members of other castes to your houses ?

Yes/No

2. Do you have any objection in interdining with any of the following castes ?

(*i*) Nairs Yes/No
(*ii*) Nadars Yes/No
(*iii*) Pulayas Yes/No

3. If you invite members belonging to other castes for feasts in your family, how do you arrange for providing their meals ?
No separate arrangement/Separate arrangement for each caste/If any other, please specify.

4. Did your following relatives use to invite other castes for family functions ?

(*i*) Parents Yes/No
(*ii*) Grand parents Yes/No
(*iii*) Great grand parents Yes/No

5. Do you allow the following people to enter into your kitchen ?

(*i*) Nadars Yes/No
(*ii*) Nairs Yes/No
(*iii*) Pulayas Yes/No

6. Do you think that each caste should have its own separate places of worship ?

Yes/No

7. What do you think of the human nature with reference to your relations ?

(*a*) Within your caste
(*b*) With other castes

(*c*) Within your class
(*d*) With other classes

8. Do you believe in supernatural powers ?

Yes/No

9. Do you invoke supernatural blessings at the time of agricultural operations and other occupational pursuits ?

Yes/No

10. How do you look forward to your future life ?
(*a*) Optimistic/or confident
(*b*) Pessimistic/or uncertain

11. Which do you believe in the factor shaping your life ? One's own effort/One's own effort and fate/fate alone.

APPENDIX II

Schedule for the Collection of General Data and Interview Guide

Information is to be collected about the following aspects :

1. *The layout of the villages*
   The location of the three villages, its boundaries, nearest towns and routes to it. The distinct features of the villages ; irrigation sources ; food grains especially paddy field. Lay out of the households ; residential clustering of each caste and class. Means of transport and communication within the village.

2. *Historical background*
   Village settlement in the early days. Historical facts and legends about the origin of the villages.

3. *Institutions of the villages*
   Family marriage and religious institutions like Church, Mosque and Temples. Medical facilities, post office, voluntary associations, schools, Panchayat Offices and marketing centres.

4. *Religious aspects*
   Feasts and festivals of the religious institutions, Religious celebrations like Onam, Deepavali, Easter, Xmas, etc.

5. *Social aspects*
   Marriages and other social festivals like one on the occasion of harvest, death etc.

6. *Inter-group relations*
   Unique events if any revealing inter-class and inter-caste relations. Inter-group conflict areas.

7. *Individual aspects*
   Influential persons of the villages, from all caste and class groups.

GLOSSARY

Adiyan : An outcaste person who is attached to the landlord as a semi-slave.

Agastheswaram : A small village in South Travancore.

Ambalapuzha : A town in Kerala

Anna Dravida Munnetta Kazhagam : A political party in Tamil Nadu.

Asari : Carpenter ; A Hindu occupational Caste (Polluting).

Avatharas : Incarnations of God Vishnu.

Cheri : The locality where Pulayas live.

Desavazhi : Feudal Chieftain of a Desam (A Taluk).

Dravida Munnetta Kazhagam : A Political Party in Tamil Nadu.

Illum : A sub-caste among the Nairs of Kerala.

Kalari : School in traditional Kerala where military training used to be imparted.

Kallasari : Mason ; A Hindu occupational caste.

Kammalan : Artisan Castes.

Karanavan : The Head of a Nair joint family.

Karayogam : A Nair association.

Kiriyam : A sub-caste among Nairs.

Kollan : Blacksmith ; A Hindu occupational caste.

Malayalam : Language spoken in Kerala.

Mara Asari : Carpenter ; A Hindu occupational caste in Kerala.

Mussari : Brasier ; A Hindu occupational caste in Kerala.

Naduvazhi : The chief of a 'Nad' (A District).

Nair Service Society : An association of Nairs.
Swarupi : A sub-caste among Nairs.
Tamil : A language spoken in South Travancore.
Thamiravaruni : A river in South Travancore.
Thovala : A small town in South Travancore.
Veluthedan : Washerman ; A low caste Hindu in Kerala.
Vilakkithala Nair : Barbar ; A low caste Hindu in Kerala.

BIBLIOGRAPHY

Aiyer, L.K. Ananthakrishnan : "The Cochin Tribes and Castes", Vol. I, Cochin, 1909.

Aron, Raymond : "Main Currents in Sociological Thought", Vol. II, Lowe and Brydone Ltd , London, 1968.

Avineri Shlomo : "The Social and Political Thought in Karl Marx", Cambridge University Press, 1968.

Bahadur Mah : "A Story of Indian Culture", Vishveshwaranand Vedic Research Institute, Hoshiarpur, 1956.

Blout, E.A.H. : "The Caste System of Northern India", Oxford University Press, 1931.

Bogardus, E.S. : "The Development of Social Thought", Longmans Green & Co., Inc., 1960.

Bottomore T.B. and Maximilien Rubel : "Karl Marx : Selected Essays in Sociology and Social Philosophy", G.A. Watts & Co. Ltd., London.

Bredemeier, Henry C. and Stephenson Richard M. : "The Analysis of Social System" Holt, Rinehart and Winston, Inc., 1962.

Chhibbar, Y.P. : "From Caste to Class : A Study of the Indian Middle Classes" Associated Publishing House, New Delhi—5, 1968.

Caldwell, Robert : "The Tinnevelly Shannars : A Sketch of their Religion ; and their Moral condition and characteristics as a caste", Christian Knowledge Society Press, Madras, 1849.

Davis, Kingsley : "Human Society", New York, The Macmillan Company, 1849.

Desai, A.R. (Ed.) : "Rural Sociology in India", The Indian Society of Agricultural Economics, Bombay, 1961.

Desai, A.R. (Ed.) : "Rural India in Translation", Popular Book Depot, Bombay—7, 1961.

Dube, S.C. : "Indian village", Cornell University Press, New York, 1965.

Dubois, Abbe J.A. (Translated by Henry K. Beauchamp, C.I.E.): "Hindu Manners, Customs and Ceremonies", Third Edition, Clarendon Press, Oxford, 1972.

Dumont, Lewis and Pocock, D. (Eds.) : "Contribution to Indian Sociology", No. 2, 1958.

Durkheim, Emile : "The Elementary Forms of Religious Life" (Translated by Joseph Vard Savain), London, George Allen & Unwin, 1915. "Suicide" Lowe and Brydone Ltd., London, 1968.

Fredman, Maurice (Ed.) : "Social Organization", Essays presented to Raymond Firth, Frank Cass & Co. Ltd., 1967.

Hivale, Shamrao : "The Pardhans of the Upper Narbada Valley", Oxford University Press, Bombay, 1946.

Hodges (Jr), Harold, M : "Social Stratification : Class in America", Schenkman Publishing Co., 1969.

Hutton, J.H. : "Caste in India", Oxford University Press, 1962.

Ishwaran, K. : "Tradition and Economy in Village India", London, Routledge & Kegan Paul, 1966.

Jackson, J.A. (Ed.) : "Sociological Studies-I-Social Stratification", Cambridge University Press, 1968.

Jordan, Z.A. (Ed.) : "Karl Marx : Economy, Class and Social Evaluation", Michael Joseph Ltd., 1971.

Joshi, P.C. (Ed.) : "Homage to Karl Marx : A Symposium", People's Publishing House, New Delhi, 1969.

Kapadia, K.M. : "Hindu Kinship : An Important Chapter in Hindu Social History", The Popular Book Depot, 1947.

Korn Hauser, W. Arthur (Ed.) : "Problems of Power in American Democracy", Detriot—Wayne State University Press, 1859.

Lapiere, Richard, T. : "Social Change", McGraw Hill Book Co., 1965.

Leach, E.R. (Ed.) : "Aspects of Caste in South India, Ceylon and North West Pakistan", Cambridge University Press, 1960.

Lewis, Oscar : "Village Life in Northern India", Urbana, University of Illinois Press, 1958.

Little John, James : "Social Stratification", George Allen & Unwin Ltd., London, 1972.

Madan, G.R. : "Changing Pattern of Indian Village", S. Chand & Co., Punjab, 1959.

Marriot, Mokim : "Caste Ranking and Community Structure in Five Regions of India and Pakistan", Deccan College, Poona, 1953.

Mathur K.S. & Agrawal B.C. (Eds.) : "Tribe, Caste and Peasantry", Ethnographic and Folk Culture Society, Lucknow, 1974.

Mayer, Adrian, C. : "Caste and Kinship in Central India", University of California Press, Berkeley, 1960.

Mayer, K.B. : "Class and Society", Doubleday, New York, 1961.

McHellan, David : "The Thought of Karl Marx : An Introduction", The Macmillan Press Ltd., 1971.

Moore, E. Wilbert : "Man, Time and Society", John Wiley & Sons, Inc., New York, 1963.

Moore, E. Wilbert : "Social Change", Prentice Hall of India (P) Ltd., New Delhi, 1965.

Moore, E. Wilbert : "Order and Change : Essays in Comparative Sociology", John Wiley & Sons., Inc., 1967.

Mukerjee, Radhakamal and Colleagues : "Intercaste Tensions : A Survey Under the auspices of the UNESCO", J.K. Institute of Sociology, Ecology and Human Relations, Lucknow University, 1951.

Murdock, G.P. : "Social Structure", The Free Press, New York, 1965.

Nambiar, P.K. : "Census of India—1961", Vol. IX, Madras, Part-II, A, 1963.

Nisbet, Robert, A. : "Emile Durkheim", 1965, Prentice Hall, Inc., New Jersey, 1965.

Ossowski, Stainslaw : "Class Structure in the Social Consciousness" (Translated from the Polish by Sheila Patterson), The Free Press of Glencoe, New York, 1963.

Paranjpe, A.E. : "Caste and Prejudice and the Individual", Lalvani Publishing House, Bombay, 1970.

Parsons, Talcott : "A Revised Analytical Approach to the Theory of Social Stratification, Essays in Sociological Theory", Glencoe, The Free Press, 1954.

Parsons, Talcott : "The Structure of Social Action Vol. II", The Free Press, New York, 1968.

Parsons, Talcott and Others (Eds.) : "Theories of Society", The Free Press of Glencoe, New York, 1961.

Patnaik, N. : "Caste and Social Change : An Anthropological Study in Three Orissa Villages". National Institute of Community Development, Hyderabad, 1969.

Raj, Ramachandra, G. : "Functions and Dysfunctions of Social Conflict", Popular Prakashan, Bombay, 1974.

Raj, Ramachandra, G. : "Industrial Conflict in the Context of Conflicts in the Larger System : A Study of Industrial Conflict in Kerala", I.C.S.S.R. Project Report, University of Kerala, 1973.

Raj, Ramachandra, G. : "Changing Patterns of Caste and the Changing Distribution Pattern of Scarce Values", paper presented to the 11th All India Sociological Conference, 1972.

Raynor, John : "The Middle Class", Longman, Green & Co. Ltd., 1969.

Reverent S. Mateer : "The Land of Charity".

Richard, Centres : "The Psychology of Social Classes : A Study of Class Consciousness", Princeton University Press, 1949.

Ryam, B. : "Caste in Modern Ceylon", Rutgers University, New Jersey, 1953.

Sen, Mohit and Rao, M.B. (Eds.) : "Das Capital : A Centenary Volume : A Symposium", Peoples' Publishing House (P) Ltd., New Delhi-55, 1966.

Senart, Emile : "Caste in India : The Facts and the System", Methuen & Co. Ltd., London, 1930.

Siegal, Sidney : "Non Parametric Statistics for the Behavioural Sciences", International Student Edition, 1959.

Somjee A.H. : "Democracy and Political Change in Village India" (A Case Study) Orient Longman, 1971.

Sorokin, Pictrim, A. : "Social and Cultural Mobility", The Free Press of Glencoe, 1957.

Srinivas, M.N. : "Caste in Modern India and Other Essays", Asia Publishing House, New York, 1962.

Turner, Ralph : "Family Interaction", John Wiley & Sons, Inc., New York, 1970.

Tumin, Melvin M. : "Social Stratification : The Forms and Functions of Inequality", Prentice Hall of India (P) Ltd , 1869.

Tumin, Melvin M. : "Village Census Report from the Panchayat Offices of the Selected Villages".

Journal References

Alexander, K.C. : "Changing Religious beliefs and Practices of the Pulayas of Kerala", Social Action : A Review of Social Trends, September-October 1968, Vol. 18, No. 5.

Bennet, John : "Food and Social Status in a Rural Society", American Sociological Review, October, 1943, Vol. 8, No. 5.

Blau, Peter : "Social Mobility and Interpersonal Relations", American Sociological Review, 21 June, 1956.

Chekki, Dan, A. : "Social Stratification and Trends of Social Mobility in Modern India", The Indian Journal of Sociology, Vol. XXXI, January 1971, No. 4.

Davas Das, Rajanimal P. : "Social and Cultural Factors influencing Malnutrition", American Journal of Home Economics", Vol. 62, 1970.

Davis, Kingsley : "A Conceptual Analysis of Stratification", American Sociological Review, June 1942, Vol. 7, No. 3.

De Souza, Victor, S. : "Measurement of Rigidity-fluidity Dimension of Social Stratification in Six Indian Villages", Sociological Bulletin, Vol. XVIII, No. 1, March, 1969.

Hodge, Robert W. & Treiman, Donald, H. : "Social Participation and Social Status", American Sociological Review, October 1968, Vol. 33, No. 5.

Mukherjee, Ramakrishna : "Indian Sociology : Historical Development and Present Problems" Sociological Bulletin, Vol. 22, No. 1, March 1973.

Olcott, Mason : "The Caste System of India", American Sociological Review", December 1944, Vol. 9. No. 6.

Patterson, H.O.L. : "Slavery, Acculturation and Social Change ; the Jamican Care", The British Journal of Sociology, Vol. XIX, No. 1, March 1966.

Qutub, Ishaq, Y. : "The Rise of the Middle Class in Jordan", Sociological Bulletin, Vol. XIX, No. 2, September 1970.

Rao, M.S.A. : "Social Stratification and Social Change in South East Asia", Sociological Bulletin, Vol XIII, March 1964, No. 1.

Reyna, Jose Luis : "Some Patterns of Occupational Mobility : The Mexican Care", Social Research, An International Quarterly of Political and Social Sciences, Published by Graduate Faculty of Political and Social Science of the New School for Social Research, 1968, No. 3, Autumn.

Rudolph and Rudolph : "The Modernity of Tradition : The Democratic Incarnation of Caste in India", American Political Science Review, LIX, December 4, 1965.

Saghir Ahmad : "Social Stratification in a Punjabi Village", Contribution to Indian Sociology, New Series. No. IV, December 1970, Vikas Publishing House.

Santiago : "The Parakkunnu Palmyra Tappers on the Climb", Social Action, Vol. 15, September-October 1965.

Shah, Vimal P. : "Attitudinal Change and Traditionalism in the Hindu Family", Sociological Bulletin, Vol. XIV. No. 1, March 1965.

Sha, Vimal P. Patel, Thara and Sewell, Villiam, H. : "Social Class and Educational Aspirations in an Indian Metropolis", Sociological Bulletin, Vol. XX, No. 2, September 1971.

Sibley, Elbridge : "Some Demographic Clues to Stratification", American Sociological Review, June 1942, Vol. 7, No. 3.

Simpson, Miles, E. : "Social Mobility, Normlessness and Powerlessness in two Cultural Contexts", American Sociological Review December 1970, Vol. 35, No. 6.

Singh, Yogendra : "Caste and Class : Some Aspects of Continuity and Change", Sociological Bulletin, Vol. XVII, September 1968, No. 2.

Smullayan, Benoit Emile : "Status, Status types and Status Interactions", American Sociological Review, April 1944, Vol. 9, No. 2.

Srinivas, M.N. : "Social Structure", Sociological Bulletin, Vol. XIII, March 1964, No. 1.

Upreti, H.C. : "Status determinants in Caste Hierarchy", The Indian Journal of Social Work, Vol. XXVIII, July 1967, No. 2.

Warrier, Krishna A.G. : "The Pulayas", Mathurbhumi, Illustrated Weekly, No. 14, 1967.